Teaching on Target

Age-Level Insights From

children's
ministry
MAGAZINE

by
Dr. Robert Choun and Jane Willson Choun

Loveland, Colorado

Dedicated to Andrew Wacker, Friend and Brother in Christ. *Thanks* to Linda Anderson of Group Publishing, Inc., and to Keanan Halla and Sandra Clancy of Arlington, Texas, for their grace under pressure.

Teaching on Target
Copyright © 2001 Dr. Robert Choun and Jane Willson Choun

Visit our Web site: **www.grouppublishing.com**

Credits
Editor: Linda A. Anderson
Chief Creative Officer: Joani Schultz
Copy Editor: Janis Sampson
Art Director and Designer: Randy Kady
Cover Art Director: Jeff A. Storm
Computer Graphic Artist: Stephen Beer
Illustrator: Joan Holulb
Production Manager: Peggy Naylor

Library of Congress Cataloging-in-Publication Data
Choun, Dr. Robert J.
    Teaching on target : age-level insights from Children's minintry magazine / by Dr. Robert Choun and Jane Choun.
        p. cm.
    ISBN 0-7644-2232-4 (alk. paper)
    1. Christian education of children. I. Choun, Jane Willson, 1948-
II. Children's ministry. III. Title.

BV1475.3 .C48 2001
268'.432--dc21
                                                            00-065411

10 9 8 7 6 5 4 3 2 1   00 09 08 07 06 05 04 03 02 01
Printed in the United States of America.

Contents

Preface

A few ground rules before using this book:

1. Be prepared to learn.

It's said that "to teach is to learn twice." Don't be surprised if, in your struggle to wrestle adult concepts down to learner-friendly levels, you gain some brand-new insights yourself.

2. Skip the Stained-Glass Language.

Children start out literally minded and slowly, slowly come to the stage in their mental development where they can understand symbolism. If you really want to know what a young child learned from a lecture heavily laden with abstract concepts, ask the child to explain them in his or her own vocabulary. When confronted with unfamiliar terms and concepts, the child's mind works like a spell-check computer program that comes up with whatever word comes closest to the mystery word. For example, when teaching the Lord's Prayer, I have personally heard *hallowed* defined as "Harold," "Howard," "herald," "hollow," "hello," and "Halloween."

3. Don't Assume You've Taught Until They Prove They've Learned.

Learning that moves beyond the facts can provide the learner the opportunity to willingly apply God's Word to his or her life. This is the kind of learning that we all strive to achieve.

A final thought and direction for those who minister to children:

> Add to your faith, goodness; and to goodness, knowledge; and to knowledge, self-control; and to self-control, perseverance; and to perseverance, godliness; and to godliness, brotherly kindness; and to brotherly kindness, love. For if you possess these qualities in increasing measure, they will keep you from being ineffective and unproductive in your knowledge of our Lord Jesus Christ (2 Peter 1:5-8).

Your colleagues in Christian education,
Dr. Robert and Jane Choun

Introduction

What a wonderful, yet challenging task to teach children about the Creator of the universe. How can you know what children can learn about God and how best to teach them? This book will give you insights into knowing how to "teach on target" with children. Since the book is in your hands, you are probably (a) a chalk-dust veteran who can cut out flannel-graph figures in a moving car, (b) a nervous novice pressured into a classroom by a desperate recruiter of children's workers, or (c) a ministry leader anticipating that both novices and veterans develop their teaching gifts joyfully. We've designed this book in a way that we hope will make your roles easier, more productive, and more fun.

As you seek to understand what children can learn about God, the best place to start is with God himself. The guidelines laid out for the Israelites provide a strong foundation for us today as we seek to learn how to instill a steadfast faith in the children entrusted to us.

The Lord knew that those who were to conquer Canaan would have to obey his laws and trust his promises. Faith like that would have to be instilled at an early age. God provided the Israelite parents with some guidelines for raising their children "in the way he [she] should go" (Proverbs 22:6).

Because God understands his own design for the development of a young child, he knows that a child learns best by doing. Parents were instructed to integrate the teaching of God's laws with everyday experiences. On the road, at home, going to bed, getting up—all of these were teachable moments (Deuteronomy 6:4-7). A lesson linked to a daily occurrence is a lesson that will be reviewed and learned by putting it into practice. Practice, practice, practice is true of moral development as well as the development of practical skills such as musical ability.

God designed the child's physical senses as tools for learning. God had the Israelites take advantage of this by having them create visual reminders of great events. A stack of rocks could mark the place God had fulfilled a promise, granted a victory, or parted a sea. When a child asked about the rocks, it provided a marvelous learning opportunity.

God designs each child with needs that are not only spiritual but also emotional, social, physical, and intellectual. God models the pattern of a teacher-learner relationship. A child learns best from someone who offers acceptance and affirmation. This is seen in the way Paul related with acceptance and affirmation when he was imparting spiritual truth. He wrote to the Thessalonians that he and his missionary companions "were delighted to share with you not only the gospel of God but our lives as well" (1 Thessalonians 2:8). To the Corinthians the apostle wrote, "If I...can fathom all mysteries and all knowledge, and if I have a faith that can move mountains, but have not love, I am nothing" (1 Corinthians 13:2). Children need you to share your lives with them and to do all things with love.

Another place to look for insight into what children can learn about God is the history of Christian education. By seeing what has happened in the past, we can better understand what we need to do today.

First-century Christian parents had limited schooling options for their children. Imperial institutions taught emperor worship, and private tutors were expensive. Many children were home schooled. Soon persecutions sent Christian scholars scrambling for the catacombs. Later, more tolerant rulers allowed the establishment of Christian schools of higher learning.

When the Roman Empire crumbled, the only youngsters with a chance for an education were the offspring of the rich and those destined for monastic life. The church had a firm grip on what little educational opportunity still existed in Europe at this time.

Then came the Renaissance. The good news: scientific advances! The flowering of the arts! Education for everybody! The bad news: the goal of education had previously been the glorification of God, but now that goal was the glorification of man himself. In an effort to monopolize education and hold onto its power, the church denounced preaching and printing God's Word in languages of the common people. However, it was already too late to stop the religious movement called the Reformation. Literacy and Bible translation spread faster than the fires the church lit to burn the reformers out, and Bible-based education was encouraged.

During this time educational methods improved. Researchers began to uncover God's design for the mind of the learner. But once again the focus of education became not the Designer, but the design. Sunday school and other Christian educational institutions developed as a response to this focus and to take up the slack in spiritual instruction.

This formed the basis for the educational system we deal with today. Christian educational ministry ranges from day-care centers to seminaries. Parachurch organizations such as camps, clubs, and publishers complement the work of the local church.

No matter where you minister to children, you can use the knowledge gained through two thousand years of Christian education to better understand how to teach God's truths effectively.

Teaching on Target is organized to allow you to pick and choose the information that is most relevant for your situation. Use the charts in the "Who Are the Learners?" section to better understand the general learning needs of particular age groups. The rest of the book is organized according to biblical concepts and what each of the different age groups can learn about that concept. We have also listed materials that may be useful to teach particular concepts.

Each age has its delights and challenges. Rely on the Holy Spirit for guidance and the best insights. Take time to enjoy your learners, no matter what age they are. They won't linger long at that age.

Who Are the Learners?

Two- and Three-Year-Olds

Development	Characteristics	Needs
Mental	Short memory	Repetition and simple one-step directions
	Literal, concrete thinking	Lessons that avoid abstract concepts or symbolism
	Learn through play and exploration	Unstructured, stimulating environment
	Limited vocabulary	Objects and behaviors labeled
	Interest span of two to four minutes	Freedom to move from one activity to another
	Learning through the senses	Sensory activities
Social	Play alone	Room for solitary play and opportunities to interact
	Trusting, affectionate	Love and support
	Dependent, but seek independence	Activities geared for success
	Fearful, insecure	Security of routines
Emotional	Self-centered and crave attention	Small teacher-to-learner ratios
	Want to please	Specific praise
Spiritual	Sense of awe, wonder	Examples of God's creation
	Trusting	Adult models of God's loving care
Physical	Little endurance, tire easily	Alternating periods of activity and rest
	Developing large muscle control	Room and opportunity to move around
	No small muscle control	Toys that encourage coordination

Four- and Five-Year-Olds

Development	Characteristics	Needs
Mental	Beginning to separate reality from fantasy	Emphasis on reality of Bible stories
	Learning through the senses	Sensory activities
	Interest span of five to ten minutes	Frequent change of activity
	Limited understanding of time and space	Lessons that avoid references to chronology or geography
	Literal, concrete thinking	Lessons that avoid abstract concepts or symbolism
	Imaginative	Settings that encourage imaginative play
	Curious	Opportunities to explore and learn by doing
	Imitative	Adults who model God's love
	Expanding vocabulary	Objects and behaviors labeled
Social	Desire to please	Responsibilities to perform
	Dependent, but seek independence	Freedom within safe limits
	Enjoy group play	Social interaction with adult guidance
Emotional	Fearful, emotional	Security of routine and rules
	Talkative, want attention	Small teacher-to-learner ratios
	Forming self-image	Activities geared for success
Spiritual	Understand disobedience	Forgiveness
	Capable of worship	Encouragment for spontaneous worship
Physical	Developing small muscle control	Opportunities to practice new skills
	Little endurance and tire easily	Alternating periods of activity and rest
	Developing large muscles	Room and opportunity to move around

First- Through Third-Graders

Development	Characteristics	Needs
Mental	Enjoy dramatic play	Drama activities to teach Bible truths
	Creative	Varied opportunities for expression
	Limited grasp of time and space	Limited references to chronology and geography
	Developing reasoning skills	Discovery learning opportunities
	Literal, concrete thinkers	Lessons that avoid abstract concepts or symbolism
	Attention span of ten to fifteen minutes	Appropriate changes of activity
	Good memories	Directions in a series, Scripture memory
	Reading, writing, speaking skills	Independent work using new skills
Social	Interested in peer group	Club activities
	Learning cooperation	Group-based activities
	Want independence	Appropriate ability-level tasks
Emotional	Talkative, crave attention	Small teacher-to-learner ratios
	Forming self-image	Activities geared for success
	Developing self-control	Fair and consistent discipline
	Seek approval	Chances to handle responsibilities
Spiritual	Can understand forgiveness	Models of forgiveness, reconciliation
	Developing personal values	Biblical standards for lifestyle choices
	Developing questions about God and heaven	Guided Bible study
Physical	Active	Frequent changes of pace
	Control of small muscles	Opportunities to practice new skills
	Voice control and developing rhythm	Learning activities, including songs

Fourth- Through Sixth-Graders

Development	Characteristics	Needs
Mental	Beginning to grasp abstract concepts	Introduction to abstract concepts
	Reasoning ability	Discovery learning opportunities
	Academic skills	Writing, speaking, research activities
	Longer attention spans	More complex activities
	Grasp of time and space	References to chronology and geography
Social	Crave peer acceptance	Guided social interaction
	Need less adult approval	Guidance leading to self-direction
	Enjoy competition	Limited competition as motivation
Emotional	Want adult status	Challenging responsibilities
	Unsteady emotions	Love, support, consistency
	Worship "heroes"	Models of Christlike lifestyle
Spiritual	Can understand salvation	Clear presentation of gospel
	Developing a sense of morality	Guidance in decision making
Physical	Large and small muscle control	Appropriate variety of activities and skills
	Healthy, active	Frequent changes of pace

What Can They Learn About...

The Bible

What Can Two- and Three-Year-Olds Learn About...

Because twos and threes rely heavily on their physical senses for information, these children need lots of visuals to accompany stories from the Bible. Tell the story briefly while maintaining eye contact with the listeners. Large, appealing pictures will help to clarify the events of the story and perhaps evoke some questions.

Even if the curriculum already supplies text and visuals, supplement them with a Bible storybook designed for this age level. Use the word "Bible," and display the book whenever you tell a Bible story. The learners will eventually catch on that the stories you tell are from the book you call the Bible. After a while, they will have heard enough stories about God and Jesus to know that these stories are found in the Bible.

Treat the Bible storybook with respect and make story time exciting. Your young learners will adopt your attitude and sense that the Bible is special. Rhymes, finger plays, and simple motion songs can teach stories from the Bible while meeting this age group's needs for repetition and physical activity. Don't be overly critical of your class or your storytelling technique if your listeners tend to wander off after a couple of minutes. Two to three minutes is their divinely ordained attention span.

Two- and Three-Year-Olds Can Learn–

• The Bible is a special and important book.

• The Bible is a book with stories about God and Jesus.

• It is fun and exciting to hear stories from the Bible.

Excellent Resources for Twos and Threes About the Bible

The Beginner's Bible for Toddlers. Carolyn Nabors Baker. Hauppauge, NY: Word Books, 1995.

The Bible for Little Hearts (Little Hearts). James C. Galvin (editor). Wheaton, IL: Tyndale House, 1995.

A Child's First Bible. Sally L. Jones. Cincinnati: Standard, 1998.

Faith in God. 4 vols. Marie-Agnes Gaudrat. Collegeville, MN: Liturgical Press, 1992.

The Love of God. 4 vols. Marie-Agnes Gaudrat and Ulises Wensell. Collegeville, MN: Liturgical Press, 1998.

Pray & Play Bible for Young Children. Jody Brolsma (editor). Loveland, CO: Group, 1997.

The Toddler's Bible. V. Gilbert Beers. Colorado Springs, CO: Chariot Victor, 1994.

What Can Four- and Five-Year-Olds Learn About...

Kindergarten-age children are beginning to separate fantasy from reality. Some will still be checking under the bed for monsters, while some will be telling teary-eyed classmates the awful truth about Santa Claus. This is the ideal time to impress learners with the fact that the Bible is true. Now—while attitudes can still be molded—is the time to hear from trusted adults that God's Word is truth.

Help children visualize and experience life in Bible times. Set up a tent. Sit on rugs. Wear robes and sandals. Scoop food from a wooden bowl using hunks of bread. Listen to recordings of music played on traditional Middle Eastern instruments. Demonstrate pottery making and weaving. Let the learners tackle simple, ancient crafts and tasks.

Tell the story rather than read it from the teacher manual that came with the curriculum. Memorize the story from the manual before Saturday night. On Sunday morning, maintain eye contact with your listeners. Keep an open Bible nearby as a reminder that the story you tell comes from God's Word. If your lesson plan includes a modern-day life application, close the Bible while you present that part so the children don't equate it with Scripture.

By now, your learners have noticed that the same Bible stories can come from very different-looking Bibles. Some children will be able to recognize the word "Bible" on a book's cover. Others will need some reassurance that the words are true even if the cover and the vocabulary level change.

Use motion songs and finger plays to teach about the Bible, but watch out for lyrics that can be misinterpreted by a literal mind. I wish I had a nickel for every time I've seen a child stomp on a Bible, singing the lyrics, "I stand alone on the Word of God!" What if we were to substitute, "The words are true in the Word of God"? They fit the rhythm, don't they? Don't be afraid to customize song lyrics to avoid misunderstandings. Review the songs and prayers you're currently using. What do you suppose the children think the words mean? Check by asking them.

Another hidden danger is an appealing storybook that pushes a Bible story over the line into fiction and fantasy. It's a good idea to add enough details to pull your listeners into the world of the story, but make sure you're still within the boundaries of God's Word. When an author moves over the boundary by adding imaginary details, the book is no longer a good teaching tool. Watch out for tales of animals that have spiritual natures so that they can become Christians. Only a human has a God-breathed soul that is able to be saved.

Four- and Five-Year-Olds Can Learn—

- The Bible is true.
- The Bible is written at different vocabulary levels.
- Life in Bible times was different from the way we live now.
- The Bible is from God.

Excellent Resources for Fours and Fives About the Bible

The Beginner's Bible: Timeless Children's Stories. Karyn Henley. Grand Rapids, MI: Zondervan, 1997.

The Early Reader's Bible: A Bible to Read All by Yourself. V. Gilbert Beers. Grand Rapids, MI: Zondervan, 1996.

Jesus Loves Me Bible. Angela Abraham. Nashville, TN: Thomas Nelson (Tommy Nelson), 1999.

The Praise Bible. Mack Thomas. Colorado Springs, CO: Waterbrook, 1998.

What Is the Bible? Carolyn Nystrom. Chicago: Moody, 1994.

The Young Reader's Bible. Bonnie Bruno and Carol Reinsma. Cincinnati: Standard, 1998.

What Can First- Through Third-Graders Learn About...

Those of you who have taught this age level can empathize with a president facing reporters at a press conference. Learners' questions fly thick and fast.

Who do you answer first? How do you answer? (I usually give priority to the child who asks, "Can I go to the bathroom now?")

When a child asks a question involving a moral choice, immediately apply a Bible verse to the situation. If you have a Bible with age-appropriate vocabulary, the learner who asked the question may be able to read a Scripture verse that applies. This is when a concordance comes in handy. As a camp counselor, I was advised to be prepared for "situations" among my campers by carrying index cards with Bible verses in the back pocket of my jeans. The verses dealt with topics such as forgiveness, gossip, anger, jealousy, and numerous other conflicts that crop up.

Try to match up the dilemma facing your learner with a similar challenge faced by a person in the Bible. This practice not only makes people in the Bible more real, it encourages learners to search Scripture for answers to real-life problems. It also helps them realize the Bible is relevant to the problems they face.

Dramatics can play an important role in the spiritual development of this age group. Role-plays involving people in both biblical and contemporary settings can provide opportunities to practice applying Bible truth to social interaction. When a concept such as forgiveness has been practiced in a controlled situation monitored by a teacher, the learner will have a basis to apply the concept in daily life.

This is also a great age to encourage children to memorize Scripture. Memorization encourages application if the Scripture is also applied in controlled situations monitored by a teacher. Conversely, application encourages memorization because when Scripture is associated with an experience, especially if that experience is strongly emotional, it is more firmly cemented in memory.

This age group is still pretty shaky on history and geography. They can, with the help of a timeline, grasp the concept that the events of the Old Testament preceded those of the New Testament. A timeline left on display for weekly review is a great help to this visually oriented learner.

First- Through Third-Graders Can Learn—

- The Bible has answers to my questions.
- The Bible can help me handle the problems I face.
- It's important to memorize God's Word so I can know how God wants me to act.
- The Bible is divided into the Old Testament, which was written before Jesus was born, and the New Testament, which tells about Jesus and the early church.

Excellent Resources for First- Through Third-Graders About the Bible

Discover the Bible. Lois Rock. Colorado Springs, CO: Chariot Victor, 1997.

The Eager Reader Bible Story Book. Kenneth N. Taylor. Our Sunday Visitor, 1994.

A First Bible Story Book. Mary Hoffman. Wheaton, IL: Tyndale House, 1999.

God's Story. Karyn Henley. Wheaton, IL: Tyndale House, 1998.

Gold & Honey Bible. Melody Carlson. Wheaton, IL: Multnomah, 1997.

Learning to Use My Bible. Nashville, TN: Abingdon, 1999.

My First Study Bible: Exploring God on My Own. Paul Loth. Nashville, TN: Thomas Nelson (Tommy Nelson), 1994.

102 Questions Children Ask About the Bible. David R. Beerman et al. Wheaton, IL: Tyndale House, 1994.

Step by Step Bible Story: God's Word in One Sweeping Narrative for Children. V. Gilbert Beers. Colorado Springs, CO: Chariot Victor, 1999.

The Ultimate Bible Guide: Helping Kids Make the Bible Their Lifelong Friend. Lori Niles (editor). Loveland, CO: Group, 1998.

What Can Fourth- Through Sixth-Graders Learn About...

This group has a better grasp of history and geography. Take advantage of their interests and abilities. Develop team research tasks to build a relief map, model the Temple, write a new psalm, or draw ancient arms and armor. Be sure to ask the learners for suggestions. Explain the steps needed to complete the project, hand over the resources, and back off. Children this age enjoy learning through discovery, so act as a guide rather than a know-it-all.

Supply your learners with age-appropriate resources: a Bible dictionary, a concordance, an atlas of Bible lands, and some books on archeology and Bible history. Some learners this age are developing a fascination with archeology that can be a great springboard to their own discoveries. There are books designed for your readers that tell about the many archeological finds that have confirmed the biblical record. One idea is to give your class a taste of what it's like to be on a "dig." Cover an old flowerpot with simple, geometric designs. Smash the pot inside a bag, and bury the shards in dirt or sand. Challenge a team to reassemble the pot.

In addition to the history found in the Bible, your learners will be interested in the history of the book itself. The children will particularly enjoy tales of the Reformation: Bibles smuggled in bags of grain, printing presses buried to avoid being destroyed, and heroes burnt at the stake.

You'll need a timeline for reference and review. If you display the entire length of the timeline instead of adding new segments each week, your class will benefit from seeing the overall picture. Most of your learners will already have heard the major Bible stories, but may never have seen them in the correct sequence. The experience is a real eye-opener. For an added challenge, have interested students highlight times when God made promises and match them up with times when the promises were fulfilled.

Don't ignore the possibility of field trips. Visit a museum exhibit of Holy Land artifacts. Pack a Bible and a concordance, and go on a photo safari to the zoo to hunt the animals mentioned in Scripture.

Fourth- Through Sixth-Graders Can Learn–

- The Bible reveals God's plan through history.
- The Bible is the inspired Word of God.
- The Bible contains major figures and historical events that are important for us to remember.
- We can use the history and organization of the Bible to help us to study the Bible.
- Current archeology confirms the truths of the Bible.

Excellent Resources for Fourth- Through Sixth-Graders About the Bible

The Amazing Expedition Bible. Mary Hollingsworth. Grand Rapids, MI: Baker Book House, 1997.

The Amazing Treasure Bible Storybook. Grand Rapids, MI: Zondervan, 1997.

The Baker Bible Dictionary for Kids. Grand Rapids, MI: Baker Book House, 1997.

The Baker Bible Handbook for Kids. Marek Lugowshi and Carol J. Smith. Grand Rapids, MI: Baker Book House, 1998.

The Baker Book of Bible People for Kids. Terry Jean Day and Daryl J. Lucas. Grand Rapids, MI: Baker Book House, 1998.

The Bible: The Really Interesting Bits. Brian Delf. Wheaton, IL: Tyndale House, 1999.

Bible Questions & Answers. New York: DK Publishing, 1999.

Children's Bible Dictionary. Richard L. Guthrie. Hauppauge, NY: Word, 1998.

Holman Bible Concordance for Children. Tracye Wilson White. Nashville, TN: Broadman & Holman, 1999.

How to Study Your Bible for Kids. Kay Arthur and Janna Arndt. Eugene, OR: Harvest House, 2000.

I Want to Know About the Bible. Rick Osborne. Grand Rapids, MI: Zondervan, 1998.

Kidcordance. Rick Osborne et al. Grand Rapids, MI: Zondervan, 1999.

New Explorer's Study Bible for Kids: The New Living Testament.
Nashville, TN: Thomas Nelson, 1998.

NirV Kid's Quest Study Bible. Daryl J. Lucas (editor). Grand Rapids,
MI: Zondervan, 1998.

***What the Bible Is All About for Young Explorers: Based on the
Best-Selling Classic by Henrietta Mears.*** Frances Blankenbaker
and Henrietta C. Mears. Ventura, CA: Gospel Light, 1998.

The Young Reader's Bible. Introduction by Charles C. Ryrie. World
Bible, 1999.

Teaching Aims

By the time the learner is ready for junior high,
he or she should be able to

- explain in his or her own words why the Bible is true.
- explain in his or her own words the process of inspiration.
- describe how the Bible is organized.
- describe the kinds of books contained in the Bible.
- identify some major figures and historical events of the Bible.
- understand the connection between the Old Testament
  promise of a Savior and the New Testament accounts of the
  life of Christ.

What Can They Learn About...

God the Father

What Can Two- and Three-Year-Olds Learn About...

God the Father

Very young children need to hear words linked to actions and objects. This "labeling" process helps build their vocabulary and communication skills. An abstract concept such as love will be defined by experiences the child links to the use of the word. A young learner experiences the love of the teacher through a smile and welcoming hug. If "I love you..." accompanies the smile and hug, the child will begin to grasp the meaning of the abstract term.

Explaining *love* is a piece of cake compared to describing our heavenly Father. If you're a child's primary source of information about God, that child will regard you as God's earthly representative. The love you demonstrate will become the child's idea of God's love. "God is love," wrote the disciple (1 John 4:8). Try expressing that deceptively simple sounding phrase in other words—words that a young child would understand. Not an easy task! It's much more instructive for you to be a living example of God's love.

The Apostle Paul, when describing God to the church in Rome, used God's creations as evidence of his power (Romans 1:20). You can do the same. Provide hands-on-experiences with nature. Utilize the learners' physical senses. Guide the conversation to the fact that all natural things are created by God.

"Pet the puppy. See how soft and warm she is. God makes puppies."

"Smell the pretty flowers. God made the flowers."

"Feel the rain. How does it feel? Who makes the rain fall?"

One Sunday our class of three-year-olds was visited by a waddling, white duck brought from the farm of a church member. The children were able to feel, hear, and even smell a part of God's creation. Those kids will never forget that God makes ducks. It was a messy, but memorable, morning.

The young child loves to hug puppies, smell flowers, feel rain, and chase ducks. Most of all, they love being the center of the universe. They command attention. Their favorite word is their own name. Anything the young child sees is his or her property, including the toy tightly clenched in the hand of a playmate. Favorite stories are the ones that feature the child. The truth that God took the time to design him or her will affirm the child's own high self-esteem. One way to accomplish this is to use a lot of songs and finger plays that have words like "God made your hands and God made your toes. God made your eyes and

God made your nose." It's simple yet effective in teaching the truth of God's design of each child. You'll get tired of it long before the child will.

Two- and Three-Year-Olds Can Learn–

- God is real.
- God loves me.
- God made me.
- God made the world.

An Excellent Resource for Twos and Threes About God the Father

My God Is So Great! Jody Brolsma (editor). Loveland, CO: Group, 1999.

What Can Four- and Five-Year-Olds Learn About...

Most children this age can develop a positive image of their heavenly Father. If they have found their own fathers or other significant adult males to be protective and trustworthy, these characteristics will be projected onto their idea of God the Father. The absence of a loving male adult does not negate the love of important female figures in the child's life. It simply means that the child has no reference point for the term "loving father."

Examples of God's character can also be found in nature. Four- and five-year-olds have been around long enough to be aware of cycles in the natural world. Bleak winters turn to blossoming springs. Summer's sandy beaches are left behind when frost turns the autumn leaves to fiery reds and golds. Snow returns to signal the approach of a new cycle. These learners are aware of change and repetition. Make sure they know God is running the show. Have a nature center with seasonal displays. Read the psalms that describe God's authority over the seasons.

Children this age are usually very trusting. They can understand that God can be trusted to keep his promises. Tell the Bible stories that affirm the truth that God does what he promises. These stories can also show the way Bible heroes trusted God, like the dramatic epic of David and Goliath. Read some of David's own words—"in God I trust" from Psalm 56:4, for example. Remember that trust is an abstract term, and young learners are notorious for misunderstanding anything but concrete terminology. Use illustrations from the lives of historic or contemporary Christians who put their trust in God. Use drama to put the learners in the shoes (or sandals) of famous men and women of the faith.

The dependability of the teacher is also a factor in a child's view of God's trustworthiness. Be in your classroom before your earliest learner arrives. Be prepared to teach. Be regular in attendance. Keep your promises. Maintain enough routine to keep learners feeling secure without making them bored.

Give your learners responsibilities that are within their abilities, and then trust them to be faithful. Label your trust in them so that they will apply the term to everyday experiences. It will enrich their understanding of what it means to trust God. For example, say, "I can trust you. I asked you to remember to keep the plant watered. You kept your promise and cared for it every day." Statements like this make the concept of trust more concrete for young children.

Most four- and five-year-olds consider adults to be wise and powerful. Some adults will fulfill these expectations. Some adults will turn out to be neither wise nor powerful. Only God is all-wise and all-powerful, so parents and teachers are doomed to the occasional failure. Even those disappointing moments can be teaching tools by saying something like "I made a mistake. I thought you were the one who fed the hamster the gummy bears. I was wrong, and I'm sorry. Only God is always right."

Children may question God's wisdom when it conflicts with their own interests. "Why does God want my Grandma to die?" "Why did God let the mean kid take my bike?" "Why did God send rain on my birthday party?"

Some situations will have reasonable answers, while others will back the teacher into a theological corner. The best way out is admitting that we don't always know why God allows sad things to happen. These are times when a child's trust in God takes a beating.

It may help to explain that we can see only a little of what God sees. It's as if God watches an entire movie, while we miss most of the movie in the lobby refilling our popcorn bucket. Or as if God reads the entire book, but we glance very briefly at the cover. David said it best: "Such knowledge is too wonderful for me, too lofty for me to attain" (Psalm 139:6).

Although we need to admit our limitations in knowing God's reasons for events, we can help them see God's power. Return to God's creations for examples. It's the nature of young children to be impressed by people and things bigger than themselves. Dinosaurs fit into this category, along with volcanoes, school principals, and German shepherds. Help the children be impressed by the Creator of all those examples of power.

When exploring God's power, children will naturally want to know how big God is. How do you measure God? Children this age are still thinking about spiritual beings in physical terms. God is spirit, and spirit is indefinable in our limited, human language. So don't try to define it. Rely on examples of God's power that are big and impressive. Your goal is to make your learners awestruck. Reawaken your own childlike sense of wonder, and your learners will get caught up in your excitement.

Four- and Five-Year-Olds Can Learn–

- God can be trusted.
- God is wise.
- God is powerful.
- God controls nature.
- God knows everything.

Excellent Resources for Fours and Fives About God the Father

Does God Know How to Tie Shoes? Nancy White Carlstrom. Grand Rapids, MI: Wm. B. Eerdmans, 1996.

What Is God Like? Kathleen Long Bostrom. Wheaton, IL: Tyndale House, 1998.

Who Is God? Carolyn Nystrom. Chicago: Moody, 1993.

What Can First- Through Third-Graders Learn About...

First- through third-graders are eager to learn, but are still limited by literal thinking. Their reading skills are developing, but the ability to pronounce a word correctly doesn't guarantee that a child knows its meaning. Some children agree that God is invisible, but only because they believe him to be far away in heaven, not because they understand his spiritual nature. Teach them to see the evidences of his presence in the world around them.

Lower elementary learners are being taught science in school, where they may not be taught God's role in nature. Use plants, animals, rocks, photos, videos, and field trips in your classroom to create impressionable moments. The time to hear that God makes starfish is most meaningful when you're holding a dripping, creeping starfish in your own hands. Check out the educational services of your local zoo, museum, and nature center or camp. Some educational programs will bring live animals to your class.

Be careful not to give the impression that God's Spirit lives within nature and that nature itself has a soul. This belief is called animism. It has been around for thousands of years and is enjoying a revival within the New Age movement. God made the trees. God is not *in* the trees. We worship the Creator, not what he has created.

With the right kind of modeling and encouragement, this age group can learn to share God's love with others. By now they should feel that God loves them and be willing to reciprocate not only by loving God, but by loving others as well. Continue to label loving actions: "Doug, when you helped Vanessa clean up the art table, you were being kind. We share God's love when we are kind."

Use praise that is specific. Children are pleased to hear "Good job!" but it would prove more instructive if the teacher were more specific. "Marcus, you chose to share your crayons. That was a good choice. God wants us to share. Sharing is a way of showing love."

Marcus knows exactly what he did that elicited praise from his teacher. Because being praised feels good, Marcus is going to remember to share. The teacher's part is to continue to observe and comment. Someday, if Marcus continues his emotional, social, and spiritual development, knowing that kindness pleases God will be reward enough.

To encourage social interaction as an arena for teaching kindness and sharing as a response to God's love, plan group activities. Alternate between large and small group activities. Always have enough adults to monitor the action and guide the conversation. To create a bond between the students and specific teachers, let the Bible lesson always be taught to the same small groups by the same adults. Occasionally, for activities such as games and centers, use arbitrary criteria like shoe color or first initials to form different small groups each week. This gives children the chance to use their developing social skills in new settings.

A personal touch is important when teaching children to share God's love beyond the classroom. Organizations that serve the aged, sick, or homeless may not be receptive to young children who want to visit their facilities. Don't let that stop you from helping these people in ways that do not involve personal contact, but always continue to seek out avenues for face-to-face encounters. A remarkable family in one school spends every Thanksgiving helping serve dinner at the local homeless shelter. The needy are served, God is served, and the family returns home with renewed gratitude for God's blessings. This kind of activity can be planned for your classroom as well.

First- Through Third-Graders Can Learn–

- God is loving.
- I can share God's love with others.
- God is real and with me.
- God has a plan for my life.

Excellent Resources for First- Through Third-Graders About God the Father

Helping Children Know God. Christine Yount. Loveland, CO: Group, 1995.

101 Questions Children Ask About God. David R. Veerman et al. Wheaton, IL: Tyndale House, 1992.

What Can Fourth- Through Sixth-Graders Learn About...

God the Father

This age group has the intellectual capacity to grasp the content of what has—up to now—been a black hole of speculation. The average fourth- through sixth-grader can, at last, understand abstract concepts. The physics of gravity. The beauty of art. The value of self-control. The spiritual nature of God (John 4:24). The credible existence of the unseen is now a part of the child's thinking. This does not mean that younger children cannot believe in God's existence. Younger children have a simplified perspective on the nature of God.

Object lessons have begun to make sense. Symbols have taken on meaning. The rituals of the worship service reveal their purpose. These learners may no longer display eye-popping amazement and enthusiasm, but the questions they ask indicate that they are thinking about spiritual matters. "Why does God let the tough kids beat up the little kids?" "What happens when we die?" "My science teacher told a different creation story. Which is true?"

Even if you dislike the seeming irreverence of some questions, try not to react with indignation. Saying, "That's not a question we ask around here…" offends the student, squelches intellectual curiosity, and convinces the child you don't know the answer. Lead your learners to the answers that can be found in Scripture. Build a classroom library of helpful resources. Admit that no one can know all there is to know about God, but that he has revealed himself in his Word and through his Son.

Children this age have the skills to learn through self-discovery. Teachers need to foster self-discovery by asking the right questions in the correct sequence and by connecting with the culture of the age group. Remember Paul's approach to the questions in the minds of his Athenian listeners? He began by creating a bond through his knowledge of their beliefs and literature. From that starting point, Paul transitioned into a presentation of the truth about the Lord of heaven and earth. Paul described the giver of life, who has no need of a house or servants (Acts 17:16-34). Use this example as a model of how to lead this group of kids.

Fourth- Through Sixth-Graders Can Learn—

- God has a spiritual nature.
- God has revealed himself in the Bible and through his Son, Jesus.
- No one can know everything about God.

An Excellent Resource for Fourth- Through Sixth-Graders About God the Father

I Want to Know About God. Rick Osborne. Grand Rapids, MI: Zondervan, 1998.

Teaching Aims

By the time the learner is ready for junior high, he or she should know—

- God is real.
- God loves me and everyone else.
- God made me.
- God made and controls the world.
- God can be trusted.
- God is wise and knows everything.
- God is powerful.
- I can share God's love with others.
- God is a spirit.
- God is revealed in the Bible and through Jesus.
- No one can know everything about God.
- God has a plan for my life.

What Can They Learn About...

Jesus

What Can Two- and Three-Year-Olds Learn About...

Teachers of very young children must do their best to keep things simple. Our job as teachers is to build a solid foundation for understanding of a more complex nature in later years. If the foundation work is faulty, learning will be more difficult for students as they grow up.

Avoid having to unteach misconceptions. Refer to God the Father as "God" or "Father." Refer to Jesus by name. Avoid referring to both the Father and the Son as "Lord." For this age it's best to sidestep the explanation of God's three-in-one nature. For now, let them learn about both the Father and the Son without emphasizing the fact that both are indeed God.

For this level, the age-appropriate understanding of the Son is "Jesus loves me! This I know, for the Bible tells me so." Jesus is the friend of children. Display pictures of Jesus with youngsters. Try to obtain some appealing images that show Jesus smiling, playing, and displaying affection. The cliché pictures of silent, enraptured toddlers gathered unmoving at Jesus' feet make Jesus look more like a strict librarian rather than a caring companion.

When telling stories about Jesus (and they need to be short and simple), keep an open Bible with you to help children see that the Jesus stories are from God's book. Use the stories in which Jesus interacts with children. There's so much we want the children to know about Jesus, we may be tempted to do too much. As you talk about the many aspects of Jesus, realize that God's plan for these children's development limits the kinds of concepts they can grasp. Right now, they can only think concretely. The ability to comprehend abstractions, such as the Trinity, is still years away.

Two- and Three-Year-Olds Can Learn–

- Jesus is real.
- The stories about Jesus are in the Bible.
- Jesus is my friend.

Excellent Resources for Twos and Threes About Jesus

Jesus Is My Special Friend. Susan Balika. Cincinnati: Standard, 1994.

Who Is Jesus? Kathleen Long Bostrom. Wheaton, IL: Tyndale House, 1999.

What Can Four- and Five-Year-Olds Learn About...

Fours and fives are hearing a lot more than they are understanding. Their exposure to new words is outpaced by their ability to understand them. Remember that this is still the time to lay foundations in simple, concrete terms. Keep those symbolic ideas on hold for the time being. One thing they can understand is that Jesus is God's Son. Help them see that Jesus is God's Son in a way that is different from the way each of them can be a child of our heavenly Father. We are God's *adopted* children. Adopted children are loved as much as natural children—they're just made part of a family in a different way (Ephesians 1:4-5). Jesus was *born* as God's Son and was taken care of by human parents.

Even though children this age sometimes forget how old they are and the exact dates of their birthdays, they have had enough birthdays to understand their meaning. A lot of teachers use Christmas as an opportunity to celebrate Jesus' birthday with a party and a cake. Learners will probably be too caught up in the hoopla to wonder about Jesus' age or how he could be a baby every Christmas, but be prepared for these questions. Focus on the reason for all the celebration—the fact that Jesus was born a long time ago.

Expand children's knowledge of stories of Jesus' life. Chronology is difficult for these kids; so a simple, pictorial timeline would be a helpful tool. Jesus was born. He grew up. He helped people. He died. He came back to life. Keep it simple. It's hard for adults to think as children think, but try to see the story of Jesus' life from the perspective of someone who lives only in the present.

Use pictures to show the sequence of the stories about Jesus. Putting events in the correct order is a skill your learners will be working on at this age, so capitalize on this same skill in your lessons about Jesus.

Keep in mind that Bible lessons should be directly applicable to the typical experience of a four- or five-year-old. "Jesus helped people. He wants us to be kind helpers. You can help by sharing. Jason, you were kind when you shared the glue."

When a child must make a moral choice, help him by going to the Bible for advice on how Jesus would handle the situation. "I saw Tania pinch you. Is hurting Tania back the best thing to do? Let's look in our Bible. Here's a story of what Jesus did for the people who hurt him." Use role-plays and other dramatic methods to practice how to respond as Jesus when faced with moral choices.

It's worth mentioning that the class bully might take full advantage of the child who decides to be Christlike and turn the other cheek. Watch carefully for these situations. The child who follows Jesus' example and is willing to give forgiveness a chance to work will need some support and protection from you.

Four- and Five-Year-Olds Can Learn–

- Jesus is God's Son.
- Stories of Jesus show me how I can be kind.
- We celebrate Jesus' birthday at Christmas.
- Jesus was born, grew up, helped people, died, and came back to life.

Excellent Resources for Fours and Fives About Jesus

God's Little Story Book About Jesus. Barbara J. Scott. Tulsa, OK: Honor Books, 2000.

Growing Jesus' Way. Carolyn Nystrom. Chicago: Moody, 1994.

Stories About Jesus. Kenneth N. Taylor. Wheaton, IL: Tyndale, 1994.

Where Is Jesus? Alan and Linda Parry. Wheaton, IL: Tyndale, 1998.

What Can First- Through Third-Graders Learn About...

These children may have already heard most of the major Bible stories about Jesus. They now have the ability to understand that each of these events happened only once, long ago. They can grasp the idea that Jesus was a baby, grew up to be a man, died, and came back to life. You can help these children realize that the first Christmas and Easter were once-in-Jesus'-lifetime experiences. Keep referring to the biblical accounts of the events as "the first Christmas" and "the first Easter." Remind children that we celebrate every year in order to remember what happened long ago, not because it's happening all over again.

The story of the first Easter is a good place to point to Jesus' power. Jesus had the power to rise from the dead and do all the other things described in the Bible because he was God's Son. These events are not tricks similar to what kids this age might see on TV or at a magic show.

Fantasy versus reality can still be a critical consideration for some of these learners. Parents and teachers might be struggling to convince children that unseen things like the monsters in the closet are *not* real: "Can you *see* a monster? Then there *is* no monster." At the same time, parents and teachers are trying to build faith in the unseen Jesus: "I know you can't see Jesus, but he *is* there."

The unseen can be comforting or spooky. A lot depends on the manner in which the topic is taught as well as the individual child's anxiety level.

Computer-generated fantasy is now so skillfully executed that it's become quite realistic. These kids see believable representations of what is *not* real, but the reality of Jesus must be believed without concrete proof. Jesus himself commented on this very point. Remember his response to Thomas' doubt? "Because you have seen me, you have believed; blessed are those who have not seen and yet have believed" (John 20:29).

Use drama to bring the stories of Jesus to life. Add costumes and props. Use a classroom situation as a teachable moment to tell an applicable account of something Jesus taught. "Teacher! I put a dollar in the offering basket and Rachel only put in a nickel!" This is not a time to offer a refund just to keep the peace. Tell the story of the widow's mite.

At this age, a child is capable of memorizing simply stated, age-appropriate Bible verses. Be sure to include the words of Jesus in your selection of verses so that his words will be readily remembered when the child faces difficult situations.

First- Through Third-Graders Can Learn–

- Jesus died, but he came back to life.
- Jesus had power to do all the things described in the Bible because he is God's Son.
- Jesus is real, even though I can't see him.
- Jesus' words can help me know what to do and are important enough to memorize.

What Can Fourth- Through Sixth-Graders Learn About...

Fourth- through sixth-graders have developed the capacity to understand the abstract. They can believe in the existence of unseen realities without lumping all the unseen into the category of fantasy. Now is a good time to reaffirm the historical Jesus. With their fledgling grasp of chronology and geography, they can benefit from lessons on the history of where Jesus lived. Use videos and photos of biblical sites. Biographies of heroic Christians who gave their lives for Jesus are also valuable teaching resources. (Stories about those who endured torture and death rather than deny the reality of Jesus and his teachings always humble me. They can affect your class in a similar way.) Discuss what life is like for Christians in today's world who suffer and die because they follow Jesus. It's a sad truth, but one children should know: Christian persecution is more widespread now than in the days of the Roman Empire. The Islamic nations and communist countries, especially China, are two major problem areas for believers.

An important but difficult truth for children at this age to understand is that Jesus was both human and divine. Belief in Jesus' divinity separates cults from true Christianity. The historical Jesus was completely human and completely divine, both God's Son and Mary's Son.

Learners at this age are looking for heroes. Their heroes are usually strong or attractive with exceptional or supernatural powers that make them unbeatable. Jesus probably *was* physically strong and healthy. He endured fasting, did a *lot* of walking, and withstood the hardship of almost constant travel. But he did not have the appearance of a superhero. We're told in Scripture that he wasn't much to look at (Isaiah 53:2). You can present Jesus to these kids as a viable hero for other reasons. Remember that today's children are drawn to Jesus for the same reasons children were drawn to him in the days of his earthly ministry. Jesus had time for children. Jesus was approachable. He performed miracles for children as well as for grown-ups. He was honest and courageous. He battled evil forces. Jesus was once a child, and he understands children. He certainly qualifies as a hero.

Don't be afraid of the pain and sorrow of the account of Jesus' execution. These learners can take it. Emphasize the reality of his power over death.

Teach the kids about Jesus' royalty. Not too many nations have kings anymore, but King of Kings remains an impressive title. This is yet another reason for these kids to become loyal to Jesus.

Your own reverence and fear (yes, fear) of God can be an important lesson to your learners. No one can be forced to be truly worshipful, but a model has a big impact. If you demonstrate Christ's lordship in your life, your example is a living lesson to your children.

Fourth- Through Sixth-Graders Can Learn–

- Jesus was both man and God.
- Jesus is my hero and my Lord.
- Jesus lived in a historical context.
- Jesus understands everything about me.
- Jesus died to prove his love for me.

An Excellent Resource for Fourth- Through Sixth-Graders About Jesus

I Want to Know About Jesus. Rick Osborne. Grand Rapids, MI: Zondervan, 1998.

Teaching Aims

By the time the learner is ready for junior high, he or she should know—

- Jesus is real.
- The stories about Jesus are from the Bible.
- Jesus is my friend.
- Jesus is God's Son.
- Stories of Jesus teach me about God and how to live.
- Christmas celebrates Jesus' birth.
- Jesus died and came back to life to prove his love for me.
- Jesus was born both God and man.
- Jesus is my hero and my Lord.
- Jesus did miracles because he is God.
- Jesus understands everything about me.

What Can They Learn About...

The Holy Spirit

What Can Two- and Three-Year-Olds Learn About...

There are few lessons available for this age level that teach about God's Holy Spirit. There is the problem of concrete thinking versus unseen divinity. There is also the problem of putting too much complex content into the curriculum. It seems odd to admit that the Holy Spirit of God can be at work within a young child and yet protest that the concept is more than the child's mind can handle. That is, however, the truth of the matter. We do not have to be able to understand all of God for him to work in our lives.

The Holy Spirit is at work in the teacher of these children. Lois LeBar, a pioneer in the Christian education of children, compared teaching without the guidance of the Holy Spirit to chopping wood with an ax handle. The teacher who humbly receives the guidance of the Holy Spirit is empowered to learn and remember God's truth (John 14:26) and to understand it (1 Corinthians 2:9-12). Let's not forget that the ability to teach spiritual truth effectively is a gift from the Spirit himself.

By your own example, you can model the fruit of the Spirit. "God wants us to share. I baked some cookies to bring to you." "Thank you for putting away the blocks. God is pleased when he hears us use kind words like 'please' and 'thank you.'"

A great audiovisual aid is a living example of an obedient follower of God. When the learner is older and must choose to follow the leading of the Holy Spirit, your example will have been an important part of his or her education—and a factor in the choice that is made.

Two- and Three-Year-Olds Can Learn–

- God's Holy Spirit leads us.
- We must follow God's leading.
- God's Holy Spirit helps us do good things.

Excellent Resources for Twos and Threes About the Holy Spirit

Hi! I'm Blackberry: The Fruit of the Spirit Is Peace. Melody Carson. Wheaton, IL: Crossway Books, 2000.

Hi! I'm Huckleberry: The Fruit of the Spirit Is Love. Melody Carson. Wheaton, IL: Crossway Books, 2000.

Hi! I'm Razzberry: The Fruit of the Spirit Is Joy. Melody Carson. Wheaton, IL: Crossway Books, 2000.

What Can Four- and Five-Year-Olds Learn About...

The Holy Spirit

These children are still not ready for abstract concepts. They will translate the terminology of the unfamiliar into what is familiar. The words "Holy Ghost" might evoke an image of a cartoon ghost in the mind of these learners. If you make reference to God's Holy Spirit, try to stick with the term "Spirit." "Ghost" sounds spooky. If you use songs, prayers, or rhymes that include "Holy Ghost," feel free to rewrite them to say Holy Spirit to provide more clarity for this age.

You can describe the Holy Spirit as a special helper. Explain that just as God the Father cannot be seen, the Helper cannot be seen. The Spirit is much more than a helper, but this is a good analogy for this age level. Children can relate to this term because they are always being asked to be good helpers.

Four- and Five-Year-Olds Can Learn—

- The Holy Spirit is not a ghost.
- The Holy Spirit is a special helper.
- The Holy Spirit will help me be good.

An Excellent Resource for Fours and Fives About the Holy Spirit

The Holy Spirit in Me. Carolyn Nystrom. Chicago, IL: Moody, 1993.

What Can First- Through Third-Graders Learn About...

The Holy Spirit

Sunday school lessons will probably introduce this age level to God's Holy Spirit through the stories of Jesus' baptism and the Day of Pentecost. Even though the Holy Spirit is an invisible person, he appears symbolically as a dove at the baptism (John 1:32) and as fire on Pentecost (Acts 2:1-4). To the teacher of these learners, this is good news and bad news. On one hand, we say the Spirit is unseen, and then we show pictures in which the Holy Spirit appears in various ways. Your kids might think, "What's going on here?"

These children can learn the Holy Spirit is like God the Father and Jesus. He is not usually seen. He works with God the Father and his Son, Jesus. The Holy Spirit helps us to understand God's Word, the Bible. The Holy Spirit helps us know what we should do and helps us want to do what's right. He is a special friend and helper from our Father in heaven.

First- through third-graders can understand the character traits called the fruit of the Spirit (Galatians 5:22-23). Explain that those who are children of God develop these qualities through the power of the Holy Spirit. Use stories and drama to illustrate the meaning and everyday application of gentleness, self-control, and the other fruit. Using real fruit to symbolize the fruit of the Spirit will not be effective for many children since there is no direct connection between edible fruits and these characteristics. It's easier on the learners if the teacher is willing to skip the cute but confusing visual of a basket of fruit. Explain that kind actions, patience, and the other traits on Paul's list are things your learners can do with the help of the Holy Spirit.

Teach them that other people who do not know about God's love will want to know more about God when they see the fruit of the Holy Spirit in the lives of the children.

It's generally accepted that God's Spirit comes and lives within each Christian (1 Corinthians 6:19). Churches, however, disagree about when an individual becomes a Christian. There are also various opinions of how the presence of God's Holy Spirit within an individual is authenticated. Therefore, you will need to present the topic of the Holy Spirit in agreement with your church's doctrine about how and when an individual can receive God's indwelling Spirit.

Your church's stance may be that children this age or even younger can believe in Jesus and be encouraged by the Holy Spirit to develop the fruit of the Spirit. Or your doctrine may state that children must reach a predetermined age, make a public profession of faith, and perhaps become church members. No matter what the stance of your church, you can still help the kids label and practice the character traits known as the fruit of the Spirit. It's not too soon to start behaving in a Christlike manner. Anyone can be kind, but it's easier with the instruction and encouragement of God's Holy Spirit.

First- Through Third-Graders Can Learn—

- The Bible teaches about the Holy Spirit.
- The Holy Spirit helped Jesus' friends.
- The Holy Spirit can help me develop the fruit of the Spirit in my life.
- The Holy Spirit lives in Christians.

What Can Fourth- Through Sixth-Graders Learn About...

Learners at this age level can handle information about the work of the Spirit without needing to be told about his appearances in symbolic form. They are ready to begin exploring his work in the world.

Once you begin a list of the biblical references to the work of the Spirit, even you may be surprised at its extent. For example:

The Holy Spirit...

• was present at creation—Genesis 1:2.
• helped Mary to become Jesus' mother—Luke 1:35.
• helped the Bible writers know what to say—2 Peter 1:21.
• brings us messages from our heavenly Father—John 16:13.
• helps us talk to our heavenly Father—Romans 8:26-27.
• helps us know that we have done wrong—John 16:8.
• selects and directs Christian workers—Acts 13:2-4.
• gives us hope—Romans 15:13.
• gives us joy—Romans 14:17.
• brings us love—Romans 5:5.
• lives within each child of God—1 Corinthians 6:19.
• helps us know what is true—1 Corinthians 2:9-12.
• helps us defend the faith—Mark 13:11.

Working in small groups, learners this age can use a Bible concordance to research for themselves references to the Holy Spirit and compile their own lists. Discovery is better than passive learning because when the children are involved, they will remember the lessons better. In addition, the kids can explore reports of the work of the Spirit in the lives of the apostles and the growth of the early church.

Some children this age are already listening to the leading of the Holy Spirit to dedicate their lives to God's service. This is a good time to expose them to the many ways they can follow the leading of the Holy Spirit through vocational and lay ministry. Bring in some visitors who can relate their experiences as clergy, missionaries, teachers, or faithful witnesses in secular settings. Some ministries require specialized training. All require a working knowledge of the Bible and faith in God. You can talk to your learners about these possibilities and the good news that, as Christians, they will be provided with God-given abilities to match the Holy Spirit's call to God's service.

Doctrines regarding the Holy Spirit can differ from church to church. One point of disagreement is the subject of the gifts of the Spirit. In general terms, these gifts are abilities to be dedicated to the benefit of the church. They include, among others, preaching, teaching, leading, and helping. We all know people whose talents make them stand out from the crowd. They're gifted in the natural sense of the word. In a supernatural context, the gifted person is a Christian who receives one or more special abilities and directs them to the service of the church. Some people have a combination of natural and divinely bestowed abilities. You can encourage your learners by helping them discover their abilities and use them for God. Encourage and guide, but don't push. Most burnout in church work is the result of being put in a job for which you have no gift.

Since work groups are a good technique for this age level, assemble teams so that the natural and divinely bestowed abilities of the group members complement rather than duplicate. Put a visionary leader with a student who shows ability to deal with details, rather than putting two visionaries together. Use these group experiences as opportunities to talk about the importance of the different gifts from the Holy Spirit to the body of Christ. Use passages such as Romans 12:4-8, and 1 Corinthians 12:4-31.

Fourth- Through Sixth-Graders Can Learn–

- The Holy Spirit does important work.
- The Holy Spirit gives each Christian a way to serve God.
- All the gifts of the Holy Spirit are important to God's plan.
- Christians can use their special gifts to work together.

Excellent Resources for Fourth- Through Sixth-Graders About the Holy Spirit

I Want to Know About the Fruit of the Spirit. K. Christie Bowler. Grand Rapids, MI: Zondervan, 1999.

I Want to Know About the Holy Spirit. John Osborne. Grand Rapids, MI: Zondervan, 1998.

Teaching Aims

By the time the learner is ready for junior high, he or she should know–

- The Bible teaches us about the Holy Spirit.
- The Holy Spirit is God's helper.
- The Holy Spirit lives in and helps Jesus' followers.
- The Holy Spirit leads me and helps me develop the fruit of the Spirit in my life.
- The Holy Spirit does important work.
- The Holy Spirit gives each Christian a way to serve God.
- We need to work together using our gifts from the Holy Spirit.

What Can They Learn About...

The Trinity

What Can Two- and Three-Year-Olds Learn About...

This topic has been a hot button ever since the time of Christ. How can God, described in his Word as one (Deuteronomy 6:4), be three? Scripture backs the concept, but that doesn't make it any easier to explain to young learners. The concept of the Trinity is just too abstract for children this age. Prepare a foundation for later teaching about the Trinity by helping them learn to love God, Jesus, and the Bible.

Two- and Three-Year-Olds Can Learn—

- God and Jesus are real.
- The Bible tells us about God.

What Can Four- and Five-Year-Olds Learn About...

Abstract concepts are still hard for this age group to grasp. Children will benefit from being exposed to the terms God the Father, Jesus, God's Son, and the Holy Spirit—even though the children will not be able to understand that all three persons are God. They should be able to understand that Jesus is God's Son in a way that is very different from the way children are usually born to their parents. For now, let the learners know the Holy Spirit as a special helper, who leads us to understand the Bible and to choose the right way to behave.

Four- and Five-Year-Olds Can Learn—

- Jesus is God's special Son
- The Holy Spirit is a special helper.

An Excellent Resource for Fours and Fives About the Trinity

3 in 1 (A Picture of God). Joanne Marxhausen. Saint Louis: Concordia Publishing House, 1984.

What Can First- Through Third-Graders Learn About...

These learners are more advanced in their thought processes than they were in kindergarten, but they still have a tough time with the idea of the triune God. They should know that God the Father, God the Son, and God the Holy Spirit exist as real persons, but to discover that all three are the same and yet different is one thought too many. Teach them the stories that feature the persons of the Trinity, but hold off on using the word "Trinity" until later because it involves the idea of the three persons being the same.

At Jesus' baptism, all three persons were present. This is the best example of the relationship of the Father, the Son, and the Spirit. Remember to steer clear of object lessons. It's too big a jump from the object to the concept for this age. I knew a teacher who tried using an egg's shell, white, and yolk. She gathered the class around the table, gave a long-winded explanation, and then cracked open an egg—with a double yolk.

First-Through Third-Graders Can Learn–

- God the Father, God the Son, and God the Holy Spirit are all real.
- Our heavenly Father; his Son, Jesus; and God's Holy Spirit work together.

What Can Fourth- Through Sixth-Graders Learn About...

The fact that the Father, the Son, and the Spirit are all God can be found in various locations in Scripture. This age group is ready to hear this doctrine, but the presentation must be very clear and backed by Scripture all the way. If the learners themselves gather the information from a list of references provided by the teacher, they will be more impressed with the conclusion. Don't search through a concordance for the word "Trinity." It's not used in the Bible; but here are a few references to get you started.

- The triune God at creation—Genesis 1:1-2; John 1:1-3
- The triune God at the baptism of Jesus—Matthew 3:16-17
- Paul's blessing to the church—2 Corinthians 13:14
- Jesus' words to his friends—John 14:16-17
- The Great Commission—Matthew 28:19

This is a difficult topic, but one that cannot be sidestepped. If Jesus was not wholly God as well as man, he could not forgive sins. If he were not sinless, he could not be the sacrifice that opened the door of heaven for sinners. Jesus' power and his acceptability as a perfect sacrifice make it all possible.

In addition to guiding the learners to the conclusion that all three persons are God, teachers need to direct learners to the ways the persons differ. The Father is God, but he is not the Son or the Spirit. The Son is God, but he is not the Father or the Spirit. The Spirit is God, but he is not the Father or the Son. It's important to avoid church terms that carry little meaning for this age and to introduce these concepts slowly so the learners have time to process the information. Sending these kids into Scripture to discover the work of each person of the Trinity will help them gain a better understanding than a situation where the teacher is imparting the information to the students.

Fourth- Through Sixth-Graders Can Learn—

- God, Jesus, and the Holy Spirit are all God, but they are not all the same person.
- Each person of God accomplishes different goals.

Teaching Aims

By the time the learner is ready for junior high, he or she should know—

- God, Jesus, and the Holy Spirit are real.
- All three persons of the Trinity work together.
- All three persons of the Trinity have different roles.
- All three persons of the Trinity are God, but they are not all the same person.

What Can They Learn About...

The Devil

What Can Two- and Three-Year-Olds Learn About...

The devil is a spiritual being, and therefore a difficult topic for young children to understand. Being alert to the schemes of the devil is important (1 Peter 5:8), but it would be misleading to warn these impressionable youngsters to beware of a red-skinned, horned, pointy-tailed figure wielding a pitchfork. Nowhere in Scripture is the devil described in such terms. Paul warned the Corinthians that the devil appears as an "angel of light" (2 Corinthians 11:14).

Your main objective for children this age is not to teach them about the devil, but to help them begin to distinguish between evil, or bad, and good. Be careful what you define as bad. Some actions could definitely be disobedient and others possibly dangerous. A child who pokes a fork into an uncovered electrical socket is doing something dangerous. Unless he or she is consciously and deliberately breaking a rule not to poke forks into wall sockets, it's not a bad behavior. If he or she uses the fork to punch holes in a playmate, wanting to cause pain, the behavior could be labeled bad. The business with the socket could have been natural curiosity. Talk about actions specifically. "It's not safe to run into the parking lot." "It was wrong to disobey me and hit Amber." Never label the child as bad.

Two- and Three-Year-Olds Can Learn—

- Some behaviors are bad.
- Some behaviors are good.
- God wants us to be good.

What Can Four- and Five-Year-Olds Learn About...

This age level can recognize the difference between good and evil. They can understand that the devil is God's enemy. God wants children to do good. The devil wants them to disobey God. In the story of the Garden of Eden, the devil appeared as a snake and talked to the first man and woman. He convinced them to break God's rule. Help children see that the devil is still at work today trying to get them to not obey God. "God has a rule that we are not to take things that don't belong to us. That's called stealing. God's enemy, the devil, wants you to disobey God."

Teach stories and verses from Scripture that are easily applied to everyday moral choices. Noah chose to obey God even when others were making fun of him. Children can be encouraged to obey even when others don't.

Help this age level learn God's laws and rules, but only the ones that are relevant to them. Use stories that relate to childhood experiences, and show the rewards of obedience. These kids can learn that God is real even though he is unseen. They can learn that the devil is also unseen and just as real. Be sure to emphasize God's superiority over the devil and that God is protecting them.

Four- and Five-Year-Olds Can Learn—

- The devil is real.
- The devil is God's enemy.
- God has rules for us to live by.
- The devil wants us to break God's rules.
- God is more powerful than the devil.

What Can First- Through Third-Graders Learn About...

It's a good thing to learn to fear the anger of God and to fear the influence of evil. Matthew 10:28 summarizes this well, but be sure to emphasize the following verse that explains how much each child is worth to God. Tell the learners how Jesus resisted the devil's offers in the wilderness (Matthew 4:1-11).

Don't throw away Bible stories that feature the devil. Jesus resisted the devil, not only by his superior power, but also by his use of Scripture. This will help to show children the importance of memorizing simple, applicable verses to use when making moral decisions.

Use teachable moments in your classroom to drive home the example and teaching of Jesus to overcome evil with good (Romans 12:21). I remember a youngster who crawled beneath a table to avoid an activity. A younger classmate took advantage of the moment to kick him in the teeth. Anticipating further bloodshed, the teachers separated the two. By now, the kicker had realized that his advantage was only temporary and sooner or later he would encounter his adversary on the playground. To our delight and amazement, the injured child mumbled through bleeding lips, "I forgive you. I'm supposed to. The Bible says." The teacher helped everyone see that the kick had been motivated by evil intentions and the forgiveness by God's love.

You don't have to wait for bloodshed! You can discuss simulated situations that call for moral decisions. Ask the children what would happen if the characters in your story choose God's way. What would happen if they choose evil? Explore alternate endings, and use Scripture to provide helpful guidelines. It's best not to use Bible stories for multiple-choice endings. The kids find it hard to remember which ending was the real one. Use made-up, contemporary situations. Puppets can help present these types of situations in a very engaging way.

First- Through Third-Graders Can Learn–

- Good can overcome evil.
- Jesus will help me resist the devil.
- The devil wants me to disobey God.
- I can choose to obey God.

An Excellent Resource for First- Through Third-Graders About the Devil

Kids' Travel Guide to the Ten Commandments. Carol Mader. Loveland, CO: Group, 2000.

What Can Fourth- Through Sixth-Graders Learn About...

These learners, because of their increased social interaction and growing independence from adults, are faced with an increasing number of moral decisions. They may need help understanding that temptations to commit evil don't always look evil, especially at first glance. The devil himself was called "morning star" and "son of the dawn" (Isaiah 14:12).

Tell the stories of Bible heroes and heroines who resisted evil. Lot never looked back. Joseph scorned the advances of his master's wife. Don't neglect the stories of those who gave in to temptation. Adam and Eve broke God's only rule. David stole another man's wife. Judas Iscariot betrayed Jesus for money. All of these had to face the consequences of choosing evil.

Some children and adults who admit the existence of God will insist that the devil is not real. Jesus himself witnessed the fall of the devil from his heavenly home (Luke 10:18). Demons recognized the Son of God and his superior power (Mark 5:7-10).

Older learners can clip news stories and discuss the battle between good and evil as it's revealed in world events. Have them compare moral standards displayed in the media with God's absolutes. Ask questions like "Which evils bring destruction and punishment in this life?" and "Which ones will be judged in the next?"

Fourth- Through Sixth-Graders Can Learn–

- God will help me in my struggle to resist evil.
- Evil doesn't always look evil.
- There are consequences for choosing evil.
- The devil and evil are present in the world today.

An Excellent Resource for Fourth- Through Sixth-Graders About the Devil

God's World News (a weekly newspaper for children). Asheville, NC: World Magazine.

Teaching Aims

By the time the learner is ready for junior high, he or she should know—

- The devil is real.
- The devil is God's enemy.
- God has rules for us to live by.
- The devil will try to make me disobey God's rules.
- God is more powerful than the devil.
- We should overcome evil with good.
- Evil doesn't always look evil.
- God will help me in my struggle to resist evil.
- The devil and evil are present in the world today.

What Can They Learn About...

Sin and Salvation

Just a note before we start our discussion of this topic. Denominations and independent churches have varying views of the age at which a child can (1) become a member of God's family and (2) understand what that means. Research conducted by experts in the field of child development can tell us what the average child can understand at a particular age. The Bible tells us that Jesus welcomed children, but offers little information on the method of evangelization of individual age groups.

What Can Two- and Three-Year-Olds Learn About...

To a young child, punishment defines morality. If you are punished for something you did, it must have been something bad. If there are not consequences for the actions, then what you did must have been OK. This is why consistency in discipline is so important. If a child is punished for an act on Monday but gets away with the identical offense on Tuesday, his understanding of good and evil get scrambled. The concept that a punishable act can go unpunished is simply too much to handle. It is vital though that all discipline be accompanied by loving forgiveness. This will be the basis for the understanding of God's discipline and his forgiveness.

Teachers of this age group need to be consistent and fair in discipline. However, give some leeway to a child whose action was neither deliberate nor premeditated. Observant adults who catch a child in the act can usually know whether or not there was intent. Help children this age by labeling actions as good or bad. Don't make the mistake of labeling the child good or bad. All people are sinners, but right now the children need some basic guidelines for God-pleasing behavior. Use simple Bible verses to show children that the rules about kindness and sharing come from God's Book. Our object is to plant the seed that God's rules are universal absolutes, not just rules for Sunday school.

Two- and Three-Year-Olds Can Learn—

• God's Book has rules.
• I want to obey God's rules.

What Can Four- and Five-Year-Olds Learn About...

In the stories about Adam and Eve, children will be introduced to the word *sin*. Don't forget that although this is a familiar word to an adult, it's new vocabulary for a child. Explain by saying, "Whenever we break God's rules, that is called sin."

Keep references to sin on the level of child behavior. Because children in this age bracket are still learning the rules for social interaction, there will be many, many opportunities to teach the concept of forgiveness. Set an example by forgiving misbehavior for which a child demonstrates remorse. "I can tell that you are really sorry you threw the juice. I forgive you. I am not mad at you, but you will have to help clean up the mess."

When you forgive, don't stay mad. False forgiveness is as bad as false remorse. Try to teach that misbehavior requires sincere regret and that forgiveness, when solicited, should be freely granted. It's not right to hold grudges. By practicing this policy in the classroom, you're showing the children a model of the forgiveness available from God.

Use the story of Joseph and his brothers as a prime example of forgiveness. This is a good story to act out, leaving out the part about Potiphar's wife. The story of the prodigal son is another good story of forgiveness. When you observe the learners asking and granting forgiveness for their sins against each other, they have truly learned the concept. They can also learn that they must ask God's forgiveness when they break his rules.

Four- and Five-Year-Olds Can Learn—

- I sin when I break God's rules.
- When I sin, I should be sorry and ask to be forgiven.
- God will forgive me when I ask him.

An Excellent Resource for Fours and Fives About Sin and Salvation

I Believe in Jesus: Leading Your Child to Christ. John MacArthur, Nashville, TN: Thomas Nelson, 1999.

What Can First- Through Third-Graders Learn About...

Most children this age have already heard the Easter story, but they probably do not understand the consequences of Jesus' sacrifice. The concept of a blood offering was easily understood by Jesus' contemporaries, but it's alien to us. Be clear that God let people use animals as a kind of symbol for the time that Jesus would die and take the punishment for us.

Unless Jesus died, God could not forgive us for the wrong things we do and think. Soft-hearted children may protest that God was mean to send Jesus to die. Explain that this was not an easy thing for Jesus or for his Father to do. Read John 3:16 to the class so they can hear God's explanation that it was all done for us. We sin, but God forgives us because Jesus has taken our punishment by dying on the cross. Only Jesus could die for our sins because he was the only one who had never done anything wrong. He didn't need anyone to forgive him.

Because these kids are beginning to get the hang of chronology, they can learn that Jesus died once, a long time ago. It's a little more difficult, but not impossible, for them to see that Jesus' death was for everyone, everywhere. Jesus died for people who had not yet been born.

Be careful of the stained-glass language—church terms that your children are not familiar with—that may creep into your vocabulary as you explain sin and salvation. A term that speaks volumes to a long time church-going adult can be a real stumbling block to a literally minded young learner who has had little exposure to the term. "Born again," "blood of the Lamb," and "redeemed" are all terms that do not have deep meaning for this age group.

First- Through Third-Graders Can Learn—

- Wrongdoing must be punished.
- God sent Jesus to die for our sins because he loves us so much.
- Only Jesus could pay for all my wrongs.
- Jesus died to pay for the sins of everyone.

Excellent Resources for First- Through Third-Graders About Sin and Salvation

What Is a Christian? Carolyn Nystrom. Chicago: Moody Press, 1992.
Why Do I Do Things Wrong? Carolyn Nystrom. Chicago: Moody Press, 1994.

What Can Fourth- Through Sixth-Graders Learn About...

Most of these learners understand the concept that sin is the disobeying of God's rules, whether in thought or deed. They know that sin must be punished. Because our heavenly Father loves us, he sent his own Son to be punished in our place. Jesus saved us from punishment for our sins. That's why one of Jesus' names is Savior.

Now here's the part that can become a point of dissension among churches: When is a child able to understand all this on an intellectual level? When is a child ready to understand this on a spiritual level? Or when is he or she able to comprehend the significance of the baptism that occurred earlier? In answer to the first question, most learners in this age bracket can understand their sinful nature, need for forgiveness, and the availability of forgiveness through Jesus' death. Whether or not an individual is ready to accept this truth on a spiritual level is up to the Holy Spirit. Be alert for questions or behavior that might be an indication of the spiritual growth needed to accept this.

Some churches ask that children make a verbal admission of guilt, a plea for forgiveness, and a profession of trust in Jesus' ability to obtain their forgiveness through his blood. Other churches teach that an infant is received into God's family at baptism and needs to confirm his or her trust in Christ by public profession at a later age. Some teach that God's offer must be accepted. Others teach that it's ours unless we reject it. Some teach that only a predetermined number will believe and be saved. So know the doctrine of your church and search the Scriptures. Be satisfied that these are in agreement before you teach. The kids at this age can ask hard questions, so be sure of your answers.

Another point of dissension among churches, one that was responsible for the Reformation, is the question of "earning" forgiveness. There's no way we can ever be good enough to enter heaven and live with God. Sin can't be anywhere near God. Because Jesus took our punishment, God can forgive us. There's nothing we can do on our own to make up for our sins. Sins can't be made to "go away" by doing lots of good deeds to make up for the bad ones. Only our faith that Jesus' death earned God's forgiveness will get us into heaven (Romans 3:23-24).

If you want to try a bit of drama to clarify the doctrine of salvation, you can stage a "trial" of a sinner. Use adults as the participants with the kids watching.

Fourth- Through Sixth-Graders Can Learn–

- God loves me so much that he sent his only Son to die for me to pay for my sins.
- Good deeds cannot cover sin.
- The work of the Holy Spirit is important in the process of salvation.

Teaching Aims

By the time the learner is ready for junior high, he or she should know–

- God has rules that are in the Bible.
- I want to obey God's rules.
- I sin when I break God's rules.
- When I sin, I should be sorry and ask forgiveness.
- Sin must be punished.
- God loves me so much that he sent his only Son to die for me to pay for my sins.
- Only Jesus could pay for all my wrongs.
- Jesus died to pay for the sins of everyone.
- Good deeds cannot cover sin.
- The work of the Holy Spirit is important in the process of salvation.

What Can They Learn About...

Death

A child's response to death will depend on the age of the child at the time of the death, the intimacy to the person (or even pet) that dies, and also on the manner of death. A slow debilitating illness will give adults a chance to prepare a child for death. A sudden or violent end is both a loss and a shock. A child's own impending death is a process that can be made less frightening by adults who are able to answer that child's questions in a truthful and reassuring way. For all these reasons, we *must* be prepared to help children deal with the subject of death.

What Can Two- and Three-Year-Olds Learn About...

Children this age are unlikely to be exposed to death unless it claims a pet, friend, or family member. Death is an abstract concept, but it can become very real if it reaches into a young child's circle of significant people. Answer a child's questions simply but truthfully on a "need to know" basis. "Death means that the body stops working. The body is put away because it's no longer needed." Be sure to reassure them that the part of them that thinks and feels will continue to live without the body.

If a pet dies, allow a young child to experience the sorrow of the end of the companionship. A small animal can even be buried by the family. Realizing that death is an end to earthly life is an important step toward someday learning that there will be a new and better life for the members of God's family. Don't entirely shield these learners from loss, but don't needlessly expose them to physical suffering and hysterical grief. In later years, they will retain little memory of the lost pet or person. The loss of a sibling or parent will have lifelong social and psychological impact and may require professional counseling.

Two- and Three-Year-Olds Can Learn–

• Death is the end of the physical body.
• The soul lives on after death.

What Can Four- and Five-Year-Olds Learn About...

Unfortunately, most children this age have already been exposed to many deaths, real or dramatized, through movies, television, and stories. Since they are still sorting fact from fantasy, a four- or five-year-old may have a problem understanding why the playmate recovered from a mortal blow from the toy galactic laser saber, but grandpa didn't get up after his heart attack.

A child in my class of five-year-olds asked me why I had been absent the previous Sunday. I explained that a family member had died. The child's response was "Who shot her?" It took me a moment to put the child's question into perspective. When I was very young, babies were born at home, and aged relatives died at home. Sadly, few children today are made aware of the possibility of a nonviolent passing. My questions about death were easy for my parents to answer. Today, adults can still answer questions about death simply and truthfully without sending a child into hysterics. Death is the end of the life of the body. Death will come to each of us someday.

Don't avoid the Bible's stories of death. Children this age might conclude that anyone who dies of anything but old age must have done something terrible to deserve such punishment. Stories from the Bible of the deaths of the young and the good can help children see that death is not a punishment reserved for bad people.

I would not recommend taking a young child to a funeral or graveside service. For older children, such rituals can be helpful closures. But for a young child who watches the burial of a loved one, it can be a traumatic experience. Last good-byes said to a dead body are both frightening and confusing to young children.

Four- and Five-Year-Olds Can Learn–

- All people die.
- Some people die young; some when they are older.
- Death is not a punishment for behaving badly.

Excellent Resources for Fours and Fives About Death

Someone I Love Died. Christine H. Tangvald. Colorado Springs, CO: Chariot Victor, 1988.

What Happens When We Die? Carolyn Nystrom. Chicago: Moody Press, 1992.

What Can First- Through Third-Graders Learn About...

It's hard to say how early a child can grasp the concept of spiritual life that survives physical death. Children this age know that they cannot see God, Jesus, or the Holy Spirit, but they may not understand the idea of purely spiritual existence. The first step in thinking about life after death is the acceptance of death as the end of the physical body.

This age can understand that there's a part of each of us that, like God, is unseen spirit. That part, the best part, continues to exist after the death of the body. When the physical body dies, the spirit is set free.

Teach that after death, the physical body is prepared to be put in the ground in a special remembering place. The spirit lives on after death, no matter what happens to the physical body.

Children this age will hear stories of Christ calling Lazarus out from his tomb in a recognizable physical body. They will hear stories of Christ raising Jairus' daughter and the widow's son. And they will hear about Christ's own resurrection. These accounts can be as confusing as they are miraculous to this age group. Explain that Jesus brought the dead to life to show he was the Son of God. No one else could have done these things. He appeared to his friends after dying on the cross to show that he had power over death.

Although denominations differ on the doctrine of judgment and destination of the spirits of the dead, Christians agree that the spirits of those who are members of God's family will go to be with him. This truth can be a great comfort to children when they know that the people they have lost were followers of Jesus (1 Thessalonians 4:13-14).

First- Through Third-Graders Can Learn—

- Everyone has a spirit that continues to live after the death of the physical body.
- Jesus has power over death.
- Members of God's family go to be with God after the death of the physical body.

An Excellent Resource for First- Through Third-Graders About Death

If I Should Die, If I Should Live. Joanne Marxhausen. St. Louis: Concordia, 1987.

What Can Fourth- Through Sixth-Graders Learn About...

Most children at this level are ready for abstract concepts. Their questions about death will be prompted by encounters with the deaths of friends or family members or by natural curiosity. They have enough reading skills to be guided to answers in Scripture. Some questions will be tough, but answer as clearly and truthfully as possible. When asked questions that are not answered in Scripture, admit that there are some things we just don't know (1 Corinthians 13:12).

In a church I served, the parents of a young child dying of cystic fibrosis allowed the rest of the class to share in the process and aftermath of their child's passing. The children witnessed the slow weakening of the physical body with each visit to Sunday school. They shared in the family's grief at the time of death. Some were brought by their parents to the memorial service. The example of the dying child's own faith and that of her parents was a painful, but important lesson.

To help remove the mystery around death and to help children see that death comes to everyone, explore the burial customs of other times and places, especially those of the people in the Old Testament. Bible dictionaries and other resources have a lot of fascinating information. Compare the Christian perspective on death with cultures that believe the dead must be buried with supplies for their next existence. Older learners could share their findings in a panel discussion or debate format. Remember that sometimes the best way to clarify a complex biblical doctrine is to compare it with an unbiblical counterpart.

Fourth- Through Sixth-Graders Can Learn–

- There is a wonderful life after death for those who are members of God's family.
- There are some things about death that the Bible does not tell us, so we cannot know for sure.
- There are different burial customs, but only one way to live forever with God.

Teaching Aims

By the time the learner is ready for junior high, he or she should know–

- Death is the end of the physical body.
- Because of sin, all people die; some when they're old, some when they're young.
- Each person has a spirit that continues to live after death.
- Death is not a punishment for bad behavior.
- Jesus has power over death.
- There is a wonderful life after death for the members of God's family.

What Can They Learn About...

Heaven and Hell

What Can Two- and Three-Year-Olds Learn About...

Heaven is a popular term in songs and rhymes for twos and threes. The term hell is usually reserved for sermons addressed to grown-ups. In previous centuries, even small children were taught to obey God by threat of the torments of hell. Church art was quite graphic on the subject. While we want children to develop a healthy respect for God and to know that there are consequences for their choices, this is the age to cultivate feelings of love and trust. If they ask about hell, they will probably settle for the answer that it's a bad place with only sadness. Do not burden this age group with frightening descriptions of hell.

This age level will think of heaven as a physical place. It will not be possible for them to understand the spiritual aspect of heaven. Focus on the wonderful qualities of heaven: God is there. Jesus is making a special place there for each child. In heaven there will be no sadness, sickness, or pain. Encourage excitement about someday getting to go to this wonderful place. These are the most important lessons this age can learn.

Two- and Three-Year-Olds Can Learn–

- Heaven is a happy, wonderful place.
- God is in heaven.
- I want to go to heaven.

An Excellent Resource for Twos and Threes About Heaven and Hell

What About Heaven? Kathleen Long Bostrom. Wheaton, IL: Tyndale House, 2000.

What Can Four- and Five-Year-Olds Learn About...

The mention of the word "hell" in front of a class of fours and fives will elicit a lot of shocked faces. They have been taught not to use the word, and here's the teacher saying it out loud *in Sunday school*!

It will be accomplishing quite a lot if the teacher of four- and five-year-olds can guide them to the understanding that the spirit leaves the body after death and goes to either heaven or hell. This age *can* understand more about what heaven will be like. Focus your lessons on expanding understanding of heaven as a happy and wonderful place. Jesus describes our home in heaven as a place he himself is preparing for us (John 14:2).

Continue to use caution when talking about hell. Because they are able to understand more of the descriptions given of hell, it may be more frightening for this age than the younger ages. Hell is sad and painful. Everyone there is separated from God forever.

This age can also begin to make the connection between the decisions we make and consequences. Although they may not understand all about the dynamics of salvation, they can know that the choice to follow God leads to heaven.

Four- and Five-Year-Olds Can Learn–

- Heaven and hell are real places.
- Jesus himself is preparing a place just for us in heaven.
- Hell is a very bad place.
- I want to go to heaven.

An Excellent Resource for Fours and Fives About Heaven and Hell

What About Heaven? Kathleen Long Bostrom. Wheaton, IL: Tyndale House, 2000.

What Can First- Through Third-Graders Learn About...

Complicating an explanation of heaven and hell is the common reference to heaven as "up" and hell as "down." Try to avoid these terms when discussing heaven and hell with this age group. The risen Christ *was* seen ascending (Mark 16:19), but there are also references to Jesus appearing and disappearing without being seen descending or rising. This is difficult to understand, even for adults!

One issue that may arise with this group is the location of heaven and hell. Answer that heaven and hell are places that are different from physical places we can live in or visit. Just as these learners can begin to understand the difference between the spiritual existence of God and our physical existence, they can begin to understand that heaven and hell are different from physical places in our world.

Hopefully this age group has learned there are consequences for their choices. This will form the basis for their understanding of where a person goes after death. It's vital that this age group has a sense of hope instilled in them about what heaven has in store. This will help to keep happenings here on earth in a more balanced eternal perspective.

First- Through Third-Graders Can Learn—

- Heaven and hell are real places that are described in the Bible.
- Some people will go to heaven; others will go to hell.
- Heaven is a very special place for members of God's family.

An Excellent Resource for First- Through Third-Graders About Heaven and Hell

104 Questions Children Ask About Heaven and Angels. Daryl J. Lucas (editor). Wheaton, IL: Tyndale House, 1996.

What Can Fourth- Through Sixth-Graders Learn About...

Heaven and Hell

Since this age group has developed reading and writing skills, let them do some digging to learn about heaven and hell. Many cultures throughout history have believed in the existence of life after death. Most believed the right to a pleasant destination was earned during the departed's earthly existence. Help the learners discover that Christianity is unique in its offer of free grace through faith in Jesus Christ.

The traditional view of heaven is pretty wimpy. The idea of spending eternity playing harps and flitting from cloud to cloud will not be this age group's idea of fun. Use the Scriptures to get a more accurate picture. Bible references to heaven should be studied, but teachers must be careful in their selection of verses to avoid confusion between the new heaven and the place prepared for believers. Many references found in a Bible concordance will apply to the new heaven of the end times. Still heaven is an exciting, dynamic place.

The fires of hell can be exciting for kids this age (some of their earthly heroes may even be headed there). It won't be easy, but it's crucial to get this age group's attention focused on the awesomeness of spending eternity in heaven. Help them understand that the best experience they've ever had will pale when they experience heaven. Have them share their best experiences. Then use 1 Corinthians 2:9 to expand their experiences, making them even better—more like what heaven will be.

Fourth- Through Sixth-Graders Can Learn—

- Faith in Jesus is the only way to get to live in heaven.
- Hell is a horrible place.
- Heaven is an exciting, dynamic place.

Teaching Aims

By the time the learner is ready for junior high, he or she should know—

- Heaven and hell are real places.
- Heaven is a wonderful place.
- Hell is a terrible place.
- I want to go to heaven.
- Jesus is preparing a special place for me in heaven.
- The Bible tells us about heaven and hell.
- Faith in Jesus is the only way to get to heaven.

What Can They Learn About...

Angels

What Can Two- and Three-Year-Olds Learn About...

The biblical description of angels is difficult to teach this age group, not only because these children are literal thinkers, but also because they are such visual learners. Few interpretations of angels show them to be the powerful, and probably frightening, creations they truly are. Angels portrayed on Christmas and Easter cards are usually very frail and feminine, sometimes even comical. This age level can benefit from more biblical representations.

Because they are powerful, angels are able to guard and protect. Children are specifically mentioned in Scripture as being guarded by "their angels" (Matthew 18:10). Children this age can understand protection because they experience the protection of their parents and teachers. If you are watchful and protective, your learners will add the traits they learn from your example to what they already know of God. Because they can understand that God made everything, they can easily add angels to the list of his creations.

Two- and Three-Year-Olds Can Learn–

- God made angels.
- Angels protect me.
- Angels are strong and powerful.

An Excellent Resource for Twos and Threes About Angels

What Do Angels Do? Laura Ring. Cincinnati: Standard, 1999.

What Can Four- and Five-Year-Olds Learn About...

Some of the Bible stories often used for this age group feature angels working for God. Angels are everywhere in the Christmas story, making birth announcements and giving directions. The story of Daniel is a favorite that includes an angel as a protector. An angel helped Elijah in the desert (1 Kings 19:3-7). Angels delivered the message of Christ's resurrection (John 20:10-13).

There will be enough references to angels that these learners may start asking questions about them. A lot of angelic tradition is simply not biblical, and you need to be sure the ideas you present are biblical. It's good to go through your classroom books and screen them for unbiblical material. The book *The Littlest Angel,* for example, is cute, but contrary to God's Word. The spirits of the dead do not become angels. Angels are a different creation.

Many renditions of angels, including sculptures and paintings by master artists, portray angels with wings and halos. Wings are mentioned by Isaiah (Isaiah 6:2-7) and Ezekiel (Ezekiel 10:21), but halos seem to fall in the category of artistic license. If you asked a child this age to draw an angel, he or she would produce the typical winged, haloed, long-haired personage in a long, white robe. Be careful not to be critical of their creations, but point out what the Bible has to say about angels. When you tell the Bible stories, impress your class with the wisdom and power of angels. Be careful that the children are not so impressed that they think they should pray to angels or worship them.

Four- and Five-Year-Olds Can Learn–

- Angels are real.
- Angels are wise and powerful.
- Angels work for God.
- I should not worship or pray to angels.

Excellent Resources for Fours and Fives About Angels

Angels and Me. Carolyn Nystrom. Chicago: Moody Press, 1994.

My Father's Angels. Gloria Gaither. Grand Rapids, MI: Zondervan, 1999.

Why Did God Make Angels? Marilyn J. Woody. Colorado Springs, CO: Chariot Victor, 1999.

What Can First- Through Third-Graders Learn About...

First- through third-graders are able to understand that the angels who work for God are usually unseen. Here comes the confusing part: Sometimes they *are* seen. In Scripture there are instances in which angels were seen by some people and not by others. On one occasion, when an angel was sent to spring Peter from prison, even Peter himself wasn't certain of what had happened (Acts 12:7-10). Once, an angel was seen by a donkey, but not by its rider (Numbers 22). Lot knew his visitors were angels, but the people of Sodom thought they were ordinary men (Genesis 19:1-5). And some references to the "angel of the Lord" turn out to be references to God himself (Genesis 16).

As you present stories with angels to this age group, keep a running list of the differing characteristics of angelic appearances. The kids will be full of questions about this topic, so be prepared to answer questions according to Scripture. You can tell this group that the Bible tells us that angels are a creation separate from man, even though they can appear as people. When angels reveal themselves, they must be pretty intimidating. The first thing they usually say is "Don't be afraid!" But be sure to emphasize that in importance and power, angels are below God and Jesus (Hebrews 1:4; Psalm 8:5).

First- Through Third-Graders Can Learn—

- Angels are not as powerful as God.
- Angels are more powerful than people.
- Angels can sometimes be seen by people.
- Angels can sometimes look like people.

Excellent Resources for First- Through Third-Graders About Angels

Angels and Me. Carolyn Nystrom. Chicago: Moody Press, 1994.

104 Questions Children Ask About Heaven and Angels. Daryl J. Lucas (editor). Wheaton, IL: Tyndale House, 1996.

What Can Fourth- Through Sixth-Graders Learn About...

With their reading skills, these learners can compile their own lists of the activities of angels. Here are a few examples to get them started: Angels deliver messages from God (Acts 27:23), angels serve (Hebrews 1:14), angels protect (Psalm 91:11), angels praise God (Psalm 103:21), and angels are happy when people are sorry for their sins (Luke 15:7).

Because of their growing independence and their preference for peer approval more than adult approval, these learners may not welcome the thought of watchful, protective angels. However, this age group will be impressed with mighty angelic deeds like the one in 2 Kings 6:15-18.

Angels have become trendy in recent years. Characterizations of angels star in movies and TV shows, show up on jewelry, are valuable as collectibles, and appear in a wealth of fictional material. Because of these angel portrayals, teach this age group to use discernment to determine what fits with biblical teaching and what does not. When there's a question, have them search the Scriptures for the answer. You can even bring to class some angelic representations and challenge the learners to defend or refute the images with Scripture verses. Ask kids to examine the lyrics of songs with angelic references and see if they align with what God says.

Fourth- Through Sixth-Graders Can Learn–

- The work of God's angels on my behalf is another example of his love for me.
- Not all representations of angels today are true to Scripture.
- There are many kinds of angels with many kinds of jobs.
- Angels are not more powerful than God.

Teaching Aims

By the time the learner is ready for junior high, he or she should know—

- God made angels.
- Angels protect me.
- Angels are real, and the Bible tells me about them.
- Angels are wise and powerful.
- I should not worship or pray to angels.
- Angels serve God.
- Angels are not as powerful as God, but are more powerful than people.
- The work of angels is another example of God's love for me.
- There are many kinds of angels with many kinds of jobs.

What Can They Learn About...

Miracles

What Can Two- and Three-Year-Olds Learn About...

The older the learner gets the harder miracles are for him or her to accept. At this age, a child believes that his grandfather really can pull a nickel out of his ear.

Because these learners are such concrete thinkers, the best miracle stories for this age are about God's creations—the sun, the stars, the fish, the birds—that are all right there in front of them. Your attitude can make something miraculous out of something the kids see everyday. Put a little awe in your voice. Bring in things the kids can touch. Get an unbreakable magnifying glass to use in the classroom to examine all sorts of objects from nature.

I worked with one group of small children who began referring to God as the Boss of Nature. They understood, and expressed in their own words, the truth that only God can create and control nature. This is a good age to establish that God made the world.

But don't limit yourself to these stories. All the wonderful miracles Jesus did will amaze these children. Expose them to as much of God's wonder as you can. This is a great age to establish a sense of awe for God and all he does.

Two- and Three-Year-Olds Can Learn—

- God does amazing and wonderful things called miracles.
- God's creation of the world is a miracle.

What Can Four- and Five-Year-Olds Learn About...

This group has seen enough to know when an event is unusual. God designed the laws that control nature. When he wants to, he can suspend one of his own laws. That's what we call a miracle.

Fours and fives are wrestling with fact versus fiction. Miracle stories may sound like fairy tales to them. Make sure you emphasize the truth of God's Word. God's power made the sun and the moon, and God stopped the heavenly spheres dead in their tracks by just thinking about it (Joshua 10:12-14). This is the time to hold the Bible up as the absolute truth—unlike made-up stories on TV, in movies, and in books.

This age group still easily believes the truth of the miracles. So take the time to teach these kids the stories of God's miracles and about the people who received power to perform miracles. Always emphasize that the power came from God, not from the people themselves. Help them see the miracles as proof that God deserves our love and worship.

Four- and Five-Year-Olds Can Learn—

- God controls everything.
- Jesus performed miracles because he was God, not a magician.
- God gave the people in the Bible the power to do miracles.

What Can First- Through Third-Graders Learn About...

"Why?" is a popular question in the lower elementary classroom. "Why does the pastor wear funny clothes?" "Why do we always eat spaghetti at church?" "Why do I have to bring money to Sunday school?"

Reasoning abilities are developing for these kids, and you need to be there with the answers. The answers the learners come up with on their own can often be off base. However, to the children, their conclusions make sense.

Because this age group is always looking for the reasons behind the events, they'll ask why Jesus did miracles. A good, all-inclusive reply is that Jesus did miracles to prove that he was God's Son (John 2:11).

They may want to know why the magicians could do impressive things (Exodus 7:10-12). Help them to discover that the reason in the stories is always to elevate God and bring him honor.

They will want to know why Jesus' followers were given power to do miracles. Help them learn that it was to prove that what they said about Jesus was the truth (Matthew 10:1).

This age group can appreciate the significance of these miracle stories as evidences of God's power and respond to him with love and honor.

First- Through Third-Graders Can Learn—

- Miracles happened only with God's power.
- Miracles proved that the people who did them were bringing God's message.

What Can Fourth- Through Sixth-Graders Learn About...

This group has further developed the reasoning skills that were emerging in the lower elementary years. Their skills can be used as a way to get kids into Bible study about miracles. Miracles were not only proofs of divine power, they were pictures of future events or the fulfillment of ancient prophecies. Let the learners work in groups to match up miracles with events. Use the following references as examples.

• The prophecy of Jesus' birth in Micah 5:2 with the events of his birth in Matthew 2:1, 5-6.

• The prophecy of Jesus' ministry in Isaiah 53:4 with the events of Matthew 8:16-17.

• The picture of Jesus' resurrection in Matthew 12:40 with the events of Matthew 27:6.

Some kids this age will look for natural explanations of unnatural events. Show them that even in Jesus' day his enemies tried to explain that his power came from the devil. Older learners in this age group will enjoy debates about biblical miracles. They need to practice defending the faith and knowing *why* they believe.

Fourth- Through Sixth-Graders Can Learn—

- Jesus' miracles fulfilled prophecies.
- Miracles do not have natural explanations.
- I can defend my position on miracles.

Teaching Aims

By the time the learner is ready for junior high, he or she should know—

- God does amazing things we call miracles.
- God's creation of the world was a miracle.
- God controls everything.
- Miracles proved God sent the people who could do them.
- Jesus' miracles fulfilled ancient prophecies and helped people learn he was the Son of God.

What Can They Learn About...

Baptism

What Can Two- and Three-Year-Olds Learn About...

Although many children this age have already been baptized, their intellectual development at this time would make it very hard to grasp the meaning of the event. Since the aim of teaching learners this young is to produce positive attitudes toward God, Jesus, and the church, don't cloud the issue with too much content.

I once took a group of young children around the sanctuary of a church, pointing out where the choir sat and where the pastor stood. When it came time to point out the baptistry, the best route was through the empty pool. When asked about the pool's purpose, I gave as simple an answer as I could based on my church's doctrine on baptism. I said that the pool gets filled with water and then you stand in it with the pastor to show everyone that you have become a new person. One youngster clung to the drapery, crying that he didn't *want* to become somebody else. This is the age of concrete thinking.

To give children this age a positive attitude toward their own past or future baptism, emphasize that the event is a happy time. It's a time to experience the love of fellow Christians in the family of God. By special arrangement with the pastor, it may be possible for some children this age to get front-row seats for the next baptism and see all the smiles and excitement.

Two- and Three-Year-Olds Can Learn–
- Water is used in baptism.
- Baptism is a happy time.

What Can Four- and Five-Year-Olds Learn About...

This age usually hears the story of the baptism of Jesus as part of their study of his life. Approach it simply, but biblically. John was Jesus' cousin. It was John's job to tell people that Jesus was coming to start his work of helping and teaching. John said the way to get ready for Jesus was to be sorry for the things you had done wrong and to ask God to forgive you. Some people were sorry for the wrong things they had done, so they went to see John at a river. John's baptism in water was a picture to the people of how God wanted to forgive them and remove their sins from them.

Jesus came to be baptized by John. John knew Jesus was the Son of God. John knew Jesus had never done anything wrong. Instead, Jesus was baptized to mark the beginning of his work. It was a good time for people to learn who Jesus was. So when John and Jesus were in the river, the Holy Spirit, God's helper, came to Jesus in the form of a dove. And God spoke from heaven saying, "This is my Son" so that people would know who Jesus was. It was a very special time.

If your church baptizes children, a church staff member will probably interview a child of this age to help him or her understand baptism. For some churches, baptism is the sacrament that, along with the belief of the person to be baptized, brings the forgiveness of sins and the companionship of the Holy Spirit. For others, baptism is symbolic, done in obedience to God's instructions as an outward sign of an inner change that has already taken place.

Children this age will probably not ask complex questions about baptism, but it's a good idea to be clear about what Scripture says and your denomination's interpretation.

Four- and Five-Year-Olds Can Learn—

- Jesus was baptized.
- Baptism is a special time.

What Can First- Through Third-Graders Learn About...

Children this age will probably hear stories about Jesus' disciples baptizing people. (The Bible does not record any baptism by Jesus.) You may run into the issue of "water baptism" versus "baptism of the Holy Spirit." Know your church's doctrine. Read the Bible. Discuss your questions with the church staff to be prepared for questions about this issue.

At the time of John the Baptist, there was no baptism of the Holy Spirit. The Holy Spirit was involved in the baptism of Jesus. When Jesus went back to his Father, the Spirit was sent to Jesus' friends. That's when the questions began about whether there were two baptisms or just one. This question still causes division among churches. If adults can't agree that this doctrine is clearly spelled out, how can we expect kids to grasp it?

What the children *can* understand is that baptism can be modeled after Jesus' own. His baptism showed who he was. Baptism in any church is a public statement of faith of the parents or of the child and identifies the baptized as a Christian. Jesus was baptized out of obedience to his Father. Those who are baptized at this age, or older, demonstrate an attitude of submission to God.

First- Through Third-Graders Can Learn–

- I can follow Jesus' example for baptism.
- It's important for me to be baptized.
- Baptism is a public statement of faith.
- The Holy Spirit is involved in baptism.

What Can Fourth- Through Sixth-Graders Learn About...

Most people who put their trust in Jesus do it before their adult years. In many churches that perform infant baptism, the older members of this age group are given additional instruction and the chance to reaffirm their faith publicly. As those who have never been baptized grow beyond the teen years, fewer are willing to pursue the opportunity.

Fourth- through sixth-graders, baptized or not, can research the instances in Scripture that involve baptism. There are records of baptisms of individuals (Acts 8:38-39), households (Acts 10:47-48), and multitudes (Acts 2:41). It would be interesting for these learners to investigate baptisms of Christians living in other countries. Comparison of church practices in different cultures can help identify what is Scriptural and what is simply traditional. It's also instructive for these learners to discover that public profession of faith in Christ can mean torture, imprisonment, or execution in some countries of the modern world. Baptism is often not only an act of faith and obedience, but of courage.

Fourth- Through Sixth-Graders Can Learn—

- Baptism identifies me as a member of God's family.
- Baptism can be an act of courage.
- There are many traditions that surround baptism.

 ## Teaching Aims

By the time the learner is ready for junior high, he or she should know—

- Baptism happens with water.
- Baptism is a special and happy time.
- I can follow Jesus' example and be (have been) baptized.
- It is important for me to be baptized.
- Baptism is a public statement of faith.
- The Holy Spirit is involved in baptism.

What Can They Learn About...

The Lord's Supper

What Can Two- and Three-Year-Olds Learn About...

The Lord's Supper

Except perhaps at Easter time, this age group is unlikely to encounter the subject of the Lord's Supper as a part of its curriculum. The children who are taken to adult worship by their parents may see the Lord's Supper being served, but it's unlikely that they would be allowed to participate.

If they ask questions, it would be an age-appropriate response to tell them that the small amount of food served is a way we remember a special meal Jesus shared with his friends and how much Jesus loves us.

Help these children see this event as a very special and important time.

Two- and Three-Year-Olds Can Learn–

• The Lord's Supper is a special event.
• The Lord's Supper helps us remember Jesus.

What Can Four- and Five-Year-Olds Learn About...

The Lord's Supper

Even though children this age are unlikely to participate in the Lord's Supper, they will witness adults and older children taking the bread and the cup. They will want to know (1) What's this about? and (2) Where's mine?

Answer the first question with visuals to illustrate the gathering of the friends in the upper room and the distribution of the food. I would not propose that children dramatize the story because of the solemnity of the Lord's Supper. Focus on Jesus' request that the meal be repeated in his memory (Luke 22:19).

The children can understand that Jesus was trying to convince his friends that he really was about to die. The disciples didn't understand that this was the purpose for which Jesus had been born. When he gave them the bread and the cup, Jesus was showing them how he would die. Children can also understand that his death would be a sad yet a good thing because Jesus' death gives us all the chance to be God's friends.

Your response to the second question depends on the age that children can participate in the Lord's Supper at your church. Be sure to understand what your church teaches and why so that you will be prepared to deal with this question.

Four- and Five-Year-Olds Can Learn–

- The Lord's Supper is a serious and special time.
- Jesus wants us to remember him by this special happening.
- Jesus was telling his friends at the special meal that he was going to die for them and for us.

What Can First- Through Third-Graders Learn About...

The Lord's Supper

In some churches, children will attend special classes to learn about Communion and be allowed to participate as they get older, usually around fifth or sixth grade. In other churches, the Sunday school teacher will be their main source of information and explanation, and participation will be postponed until confirmation or church membership.

Regardless of the teachings of your church, this age group can understand that Jesus knew this would be his last meal with his friends. He wanted to teach them a way to remember him and his sacrifice. Don't try to teach about the Lord's Supper without putting it in the context of the crucifixion and resurrection.

Without the description of Jesus' death, the bread and the cup have no reference point.

According to your denominational doctrine, you will be teaching (1) the bread and the cup help us remember Jesus' body and blood, (2) the bread and the cup *are* Jesus' body and blood, or (3) the bread and the cup remain food and drink *and* become Jesus' body and blood. If the first interpretation is the one held by your church, this age group can handle it. A lot of church buildings have memorials of deceased members or staff. At home the children may see special photos or mementos of dead family members. The idea of the Lord's Supper as a remembrance will make sense to them. The other two views are much more difficult for this age group to comprehend.

Without the description of Christ's death, the bread and the cup have no reference point. Don't be too graphic about the pain and torture, but don't soft sell what Jesus endured on a physical level. The child who sheds a few tears during the story of Christ's suffering is reflecting the kind of sensitivity and empathy we wish more adults would demonstrate. These children can understand that because Jesus was a man, he suffered as any man would. Yet because he was also God, he suffered spiritual pain we can't begin to imagine.

First- Through Third-Graders Can Learn—

• The Lord's Supper helps us remember how Jesus' body was broken and his blood was shed for us.

What Can Fourth- Through Sixth-Graders Learn About...

This age group can handle the connection between the Lord's Supper and salvation. Help them see that the connection reaches back to the Passover and even to Abraham's willingness to sacrifice Isaac. Put up a timeline, and lead the learners through the Scriptures to discover that God's plan always pointed to the death and resurrection of Jesus. Fourth- through sixth-graders can appreciate the time that passed and the number of events that previewed Jesus' sacrifice.

Make particular note of the ritual of Passover and its relationship to the Lord's Supper. If you know a Christian who converted from Judaism, ask if he or she would be willing to speak to the class and explain the symbolic connections of Passover to Jesus' sacrifice and resurrection. You want your learners to approach the Lord's Supper with understanding and with reverence. You can accomplish this with lessons on the meaning of communion and by your own example.

Remind the kids this age that Jesus' own followers had a tough time with his references to their eating his flesh and drinking his blood (John 6:48-60). A few even left him. Jesus called himself the "bread of life" (John 6:35) and even performed miracles to provide bread for the hungry. These occurrences were clues to his identity, but not all of his followers caught on. Help your students discover who Jesus is and see it for themselves.

There may be retreats and conferences for children this age that provide a Lord's Supper as a culminating event. As long as a church's rules are observed and proper reverence is maintained, sharing communion outside the walls of the church can be a good thing. It serves to remind young Christians that the body of Christ is not a building, but a fellowship.

Fourth- Through Sixth-Graders Can Learn

- The Lord's Supper is a special, serious event.
- The Lord's Supper unites Christians with Jesus and with each other.
- The Lord's Supper is connected to the Passover.

Teaching Aims

By the time the learner is ready for junior high, he or she should know—

- The Lord's Supper is a special and serious time.
- The Lord's Supper helps us remember Jesus.
- Jesus was telling his friends he would die for them and for us.
- The Lord's Supper helps us remember how Jesus' body was broken and his blood was shed for us.
- The Lord's Supper unites believers with Jesus and with each other.
- The Lord's Supper is connected to the Passover celebration.

What Can They Learn About...

Prayer

What Can Two- and Three-Year-Olds Learn About...

Once they have learned about the existence of God and can cope with his invisibility, these learners will be willing to talk with him. Limited vocabulary will be the major obstacle. The teacher will need to lead these children in very short prayers with crystal clear vocabulary. Say thank you for snacks. Ask healing for a sick classmate. Be ready to jump in with a spontaneous prayer when an opportunity arises. "It's raining. God knows that the trees and flowers need rain. Let's say thank you to God for sending the rain."

Getting an entire class settled for a group prayer time will be a little like holding onto a paper bag full of kittens. Prayer is easier in small groups or individually at this age.

The important thing for this age group to learn is that they have the privilege of talking to God anywhere, anytime.

Two- and Three-Year-Olds Can Learn–
• I can talk to God about everything!

Excellent Resources for Twos and Threes About Prayer

I Can Pray. Christine H. Tangvald. Cincinnati: Standard, 1999.

Prayers for Little Hearts. Elena Kucharik (illustrator). Wheaton, IL: Tyndale House, 1996.

What Can Four- and Five-Year-Olds Learn About...

With enough practice and modeling by parents and teachers, children of this age level feel comfortable talking to God. It may be harder for them to accept the fact that God actually listens. Model God's attentiveness by listening to your learners. Answer their questions. Arrive early to class so that there's time for one-on-one conversations. Anyone who has worked with this age group knows that a child's idea of a conversation is rather one-sided.

Help the children practice good listening skills. Some teachers find that a "talking stick" or other small object is a good way to limit the talking to one child at a time. Whoever holds the stick does the talking while everyone else listens. The stick must be shared.

Before you tell the Bible lesson, tell your learners what questions you will ask them at the end. This will help them sort out the really important points and prepare them to listen carefully, just as they expect God to listen carefully.

Tell the stories of some of the prayers of Bible people and how God answered them. Encourage spontaneous, individual prayer. Don't insist that a child pray out loud so that you can monitor the prayer. You're not the one to whom the child is talking. Some children this age will assume that their prayers are addressed to whatever adults are nearby. Assure learners that you are not the one who will answer their prayers, and you are not their mouthpiece to God. They can speak directly to God.

Another childhood assumption is that wishing and praying are the same. When you wish, you're not talking to God. He does answer every prayer, but that doesn't mean we get everything we want!

Four- and Five-Year-Olds Can Learn–

- God listens to me and answers my prayers.
- The Bible teaches me about prayer.
- Praying is different than wishing.

Excellent Resources for Fours and Fives About Prayer

I Wonder How God Hears Me. Mona G. Hodgson. St. Louis: Concordia Publishing House, 2000.

What Is Prayer? Carolyn Nystrom. Chicago: Moody Press, 1993.

What Can First- Through Third-Graders Learn About...

Fairness is a big deal. If a child prays for something and does not receive immediate delivery, he or she reasons that God is (1) not there; (2) there, but doesn't care; or (3) denying the child just to be mean. This will be especially true if the child has been well-behaved in the mistaken belief that good behavior pays for answers to prayer. This strategy might work with some adults, but not with God (Matthew 7:9-11). We are promised good gifts.

Because God does not provide explanations, we don't always see his purpose in the denial or postponement of our requests. We can at least convince learners at this age level that their requests to God are important. Keep a list of prayer requests and answers. If one child's request is fulfilled and another's is denied, be prepared to help the disappointed child continue to trust in God's goodness. A list can be a reminder of all the different ways God has answered our prayers in the past. Because children's prayers and interests change quickly, prayer requests have long been forgotten before we become aware of God's answers. Write down prayers and answers for the children.

Encourage children to watch and listen for answers. It will be hard for them to grasp the idea that God seldom gives clearly audible, immediate replies. They will expect a conversation similar to the way they talk on the telephone. Teach them that sometimes answers will come as events or in the form of the actions of other people. To a spiritually sensitive child, there may come an undeniable communication through God's Holy Spirit.

Friends of ours taught their children a lifelong message about prayer and trust through their practice of generous giving to missionaries. The children were old enough to be included in a kitchen table discussion of the family budget and the amount of money that would be dedicated to God's work. Even though they could ill afford it, they felt led to pledge a larger than usual amount to missionary support. As a family, they prayed that God would supply the money so that it could be used in this way. They soon received an unexpected check for the exact amount. It was a lesson for both the parents and the kids. (The parents were more surprised than the kids were.)

First- Through Third-Graders Can Learn–

- God always answers prayer.
- My behavior is not the basis for God's answers to my prayers.
- God answers prayer in many ways.

Excellent Resources for First- Through Third-Graders About Prayer

Hooray! Let's Pray! Lols Keffer (editor). Loveland, CO: Group, 1997.

107 Questions Children Ask About Prayer. Daryl J. Lucas (editor). Nashville, TN: Tyndale House, 1998.

What Can Fourth- Through Sixth-Graders Learn About...

Prayer is a wonderful privilege. Some children are fervent prayer warriors who could hardly tell you when they begin and when they quit talking with God, because it comes so naturally to them. Others are more lackadaisical about prayer, limiting themselves to times of urgent, personal need.

The practice of many teachers is to establish a class prayer time when children voice their prayer requests and then pray not just for themselves, but for others. Sometimes the group leader will ask certain members of the group to pray for specific needs. While encouraging prayer for each other, be sure not to let prayer dissolve into a gossip session or a "let's get it over with" chore. Teachers need to be discerning monitors in order to maintain an atmosphere of reverence and sincerity. Prayer can be candid and spontaneous and yet still be reverent.

These fourth- through sixth-graders can understand that they are in communication with God, the creator of the universe. He is listening, and he will answer by doing what is best for them. Encourage these kids to keep personal prayer journals as part of a daily devotional time. Writing something down will help them clarify their thoughts. Written prayers also serve as reminders to reflect on God's responses.

The parable of the tax collector has a message for this age group (Matthew 6:4-8; Luke 18:10-14). There's a lot of pressure to put on a good show at church by praying a highly "spiritual" prayer and the tendency to look down on kids who are not as well-versed in church language. A lesson focusing on the proper attitude in prayer will help your class see that humility before God is an absolute necessity.

Fourth- Through Sixth-Graders Can Learn—

- God answers my prayers in the way he knows is best for me.
- Prayer connects me to the powerful Creator of everything.
- Prayer is a wonderful privilege.

Excellent Resources for Fourth- Through Sixth-Graders About Prayer

Hey, God! Let's Talk. Charles Terrell. Nashville, TN: Abingdon Press, 2000.

I Want to Know About Prayer. Rick Osborne and K. Christie Bowler. Grand Rapids, MI: Zondervan, 1998.

Teaching Aims

By the time the learner is ready for junior high, he or she should know—

- I can talk to God about everything.
- God listens to me.
- The Bible teaches about prayer.
- Praying is different than wishing.
- God will answer my prayer in a way he knows is best for me.
- God answers prayer in many ways.
- Prayer connects me to the powerful Creator of everything.

What Can They
Learn About...

The
Church

What Can Two- and Three-Year-Olds Learn About...

Young children's experiences at church can form attitudes that will affect their church participation for the rest of their lives. Don't cram the young learner's head with information. Let him or her experience the love of God through your care and friendliness. They will make the association that if God's house is a pleasant place to be, God must be nice too. Make the classroom user-friendly by not overcrowding, by providing adequate light and ventilation, and by providing furniture scaled to the size of the learners. Children will notice if their room and teacher are cheerful. It will affect their perception of church overall.

Be sure to guard the learners' safety. Follow strict rules for health and security. Monitor group interaction. Church must be a safe place.

When you refer to the church building, call it *our* church. If your learners will move to another room for the next year, take a preview trip with them near the time of the change. Whatever connections they make can help give them a sense of the unity of the church and its family.

Two- and Three-Year-Olds Can Learn—
• My church is a happy place.
• My church has a special place for me.

An Excellent Resource for Twos and Threes About the Church

Things I See in Church. Julie Stiegemeyer. St. Louis: Concordia Publishing House, 1999.

What Can Four- and Five-Year-Olds Learn About...

These learners are observant. Some children will have spent some time with their parents in the worship center or been shepherded to one room for Sunday school and perhaps moved to yet another room for a time of worship in children's church. They know church is more than one room.

Show them what they haven't seen. Take a tour of the entire facility. Invite church leaders to class to answer questions about their jobs.

Find some kind of service project in the church for the learners. Water plants, dust pews, or hand out bulletins. Do something to show the learners that they are a part of the church family in the same way that they are a part of their own families at home. At home each family member helps out. At church each class member helps out. The children will gradually build a sense of "belonging" to the church.

When a classmate is absent, make a big deal out of it. Have everybody help make a card that says the absentee was missed. It'll be a mess, but if you send one neatly written note on behalf of the class, it will only have half the impact. It will help these young children know that church is a place where they are important and loved. Call the children by name. Make your classroom a homey, comfortable place, but not cluttered and fussy. Make it a place they want to be.

Four- and Five-Year-Olds Can Learn–

- I'm part of my church family.
- I can help at my church.
- My church has lots of special places.
- I like my church.

What Can First- Through Third-Graders Learn About...

The Church

These learners are eager for group activities. They're still wrestling with skills such as sharing and taking turns, but they sure like company at playtime. Children who interact with their Sunday school classmates more often than once a week begin to develop a "family" relationship within the church. Midweek clubs are a good answer to their need for socialization. There are lots of ready-to-use club programs available. A club provides time for additional instruction and worship, but its main purpose is fellowship. Church sports teams are fun too.

These learners need experiences that teach that the church is more than the building where their church meets. Church events held off-site are a great idea. Interchurch events are also a way to learn that God's children are brothers and sisters no matter where they attend worship services. Bring in stories and activities about Christians around the world to teach children that they are members of a worldwide family.

First- Through Third-Graders Can Learn—
- I have special friends at church.
- The church of God is bigger than just my church.

What Can Fourth- Through Sixth-Graders Learn About...

The Church

These youngsters are getting perilously close to the age when they may decide that church is not cool. Their parents, in order to avoid weekly confrontations, may opt to leave them home on Sunday morning. In areas where children can get to church without transportation provided by adults or in situations where only the children in a family have been attending, the decision to stay home may already have been made.

These learners must understand that they are an essential part of their church. Start by making them a necessary part of their class. Recognize and praise the way different talents contribute to and are needed by the group (1 Corinthians 12:12-31). Ask learners to participate in discussions. Acknowledge contributions of ideas and service. Let them plan and lead worship times. Encourage them to write songs, psalms, or poetry for use in worship. Use dramatics, visual arts, creative movement, and any other techniques that might draw out a reluctant participant. By using the learners themselves as resources, you will promote their "ownership" of their church.

At home, family members have responsibilities that are carried out for the benefit of the unit. Church family members should have the same feeling of belonging and responsibility toward this age group.

Fourth- Through Sixth-Graders Can Learn—

- The body of Christ includes me.
- My special gifts and talents are needed by my church.

An Excellent Resource for Fourth- Through Sixth-Graders About the Church

I Want to Know About the Church. Rick Osborne. Grand Rapids, MI: Zondervan, 1998.

Teaching Aims

By the time the learner is ready for junior high, he or she should know—

- My church is a happy place, and has special places for me.
- I'm an important part of my church family.
- The church of God is larger than just my own church.
- The body of Christ includes me.
- Church is a place for special relationships.
- God has given me special gifts that I can use in my church.

What Can They Learn About...

The Last Days

What Can Two- and Three-Year-Olds Learn About...

These learners have no concept of time. To tell them that the world will come to an end "soon" will mean nothing. If the event doesn't happen immediately after you say it, they'll forget all about it. Concentrate your efforts on nurturing the idea that God loves each learner and is in control of everything. That's a great foundation on which to build lessons in years to come. Children who know God loves them will later easily accept that God will someday take them to his home to live.

Even to say "Jesus is coming back" will cause confusion. Haven't we been telling these learners that Jesus is close to them? Where did he go? Come back from where? Save teaching last-day beliefs—which will involve difficult questions and answers—until the children are older.

Two- and Three-Year-Olds Can Learn—
• God loves me and is in control of everything.

What Can Four- and Five-Year-Olds Learn About...

Jesus told his disciples that even he didn't know the exact time of his return. These learners can handle the idea that Jesus will come back someday, but they will continually ask about when it will happen. Anyone who has taken young children on a long car trip knows the agony of "Are we there yet?"

Instead of making them paranoid with predictions of the political and natural disasters, emphasize the love of God. God won't forget those who trust him. All Christians will have brand-new bodies that will never wear out. We will have a wonderful new home in a beautiful city. We won't even need a light bulb—or the sun, moon, or stars—because God will be there. In his light it will never be dark.

Comfort children with the fact that all Christians will be together as God's family in a place Jesus is preparing. They will wait with anticipation the same way they wait for Christmas. We, as adults, tend to trust the calendar to show the difference between a day and a thousand years. At this age level, it just doesn't matter. They know it's going to come along eventually, but they have no idea how soon.

Four- and Five-Year-Olds Can Learn—

• God will take me to live with him someday.
• Living with God will be wonderful and exciting.

An Excellent Resource for Fours and Fives About the Last Days

When Jesus Comes Back. Carolyn Nystrom. Chicago: Moody Press, 1994.

What Can First- Through Third-Graders Learn About...

The doctrine of the last days has more prominence in some denominations than in others. Some learners this age will be inundated with information, while others may remain ignorant about the whole idea. Test the understanding of the content you present by asking kids to tell you what they've learned—in their own words.

The biblical prophecy of the last days confuses most adults. There can be no doubt that the words are true, but there's a lot of disagreement about what they mean. Don't get into a study of comparative interpretations with these kids. Just give them the basics. After God defeats the devil and his followers, they will be punished forever. God will take away the heaven and earth that exist now and make a new heaven and earth. Christ's followers will all have new bodies and a wonderful new home. It's something wonderful to look forward to. When you read the letters of the apostles, you can see that early Christians could hardly wait. Try to instill this same enthusiasm in your children.

First- Through Third-Graders Can Learn—

• Someday there will be punishment for those who have not trusted in Jesus and a terrific new home for Jesus' followers.
• The Bible tells about the events that will happen at the end of this age.

What Can Fourth- Through Sixth-Graders Learn About...

These kids may already understand that there will be an end to this world, and a new beginning in the New Jerusalem, so what else is there to talk about?

In Acts, Luke reports the ascension of the resurrected Christ. The disciples are standing around, staring at the clouds where Jesus has just disappeared. Two men in white ask them why they're just standing around. After all, Jesus will be back. (Acts 1:8-11).

Don't just stand there—do something! That's our message to this age level. They need to know what to do while we wait. Peter's letters give specifics about living a godly life. The gospels record the Great Commission. There's a lot to be done. There are a lot of parables to use in teaching this concept. Among the kingdom parables are the stories of the faithful servant (Matthew 24:45-51), the ten virgins (Matthew 25:1-13), and the ten talents (Matthew 25:14-30).

Older students ought to learn what Christ had to say about deception during the last days (Matthew 24:4-6). Tragedies involving cult groups with self-proclaimed leaders are in the news on a regular basis. Discuss the false claims of cult groups with older learners who demonstrate intellectual and spiritual maturity. The initial approach of a cult recruiter is usually warm, accepting, and fuzzy—fuzzy about the facts. Before a confused young person can discern the flaws in the cult's doctrine, he or she has been charmed by the attention and affection offered.

Another reason for the encouragement of Bible study among these learners is to develop the habit of searching the Scripture for answers to questions. A young person who knows Scripture and how to discern its meaning will compare cult doctrine with God's Word and discover the deception.

Fourth- Through Sixth-Graders Can Learn—

- I can serve God while I wait for him.
- I need to learn the Bible's truth so that I can judge the truth of the teachings that I encounter.

Teaching Aims

By the time the learner is ready for junior high, he or she should know—

- God loves me and is in control of everything.
- God will take me to live with him someday.
- Living with God will be wonderful and exciting.
- There will be punishment for those who have not trusted in Jesus and a terrific new home for the followers of Jesus.
- I need to serve God while I wait for him.
- I need to know the Bible's truths so that I can judge the truth of other teachings that I encounter.